An Introduction to Spatial Planning in the Netherlands

This book provides an introduction to spatial planning in the Netherlands. It explores the academic underpinnings of the discipline and its practical implications, making use of insights on planning practices from the Netherlands. As an academic book with relevance for spatial planning teaching and practice, the relation between planning practice and planning as an academic discipline are discussed.

A key analytical concept is introduced to discuss the different dimensions of planning: the planning triangle. This framework helps to bridge the strategic and conceptual elements of planning with its realization. The object, process, and context of planning and its relations are discussed. The core of the academic discipline and profession of spatial planning entails looking (far) into the future, stimulating discussion, formulating a desired future direction through an informal and collective planning process, and then formalizing and placing current action into that future perspective. In that sense, spatial planning can be understood as the strategic organization of hopes and expectations.

As a study book it is suitable for students of planning at various universities, but also for students in higher professional education. For those involved in the professional field of spatial planning, this book offers a sound foundation.

Dr. Patrick Witte is Assistant Professor in Urban and Regional Planning at the Department of Human Geography and Planning, Faculty of Geosciences, Utrecht University (the Netherlands). His research focuses on integrated spatial planning and transport infrastructure systems, with a particular focus on digital transformations of cities (planning support, smart governance, smart mobility). He is the programme coordinator of the master's programme in spatial planning, that was awarded the AESOP Certificate of Quality for Excellence in Education (2019–2024). He is coordinating and teaching courses in the master's programme in spatial planning and in the bachelor's programme in human geography and planning.

Dr. Thomas Hartmann is the Chair of Land Policy and Land Management at the School of Planning, Technical University of Dortmund (Germany) and also affiliated with the Czech University Jan Evangelista Purkyne (UJEP) in Usti nad Labem, Faculty of Social and Economic Studies. His research focuses on strategies of municipal land policy and the relation of flood risk management and property rights. He is also president of the International Academic Association on Planning, Law, and Property Rights.

An Introduction to Spatial Planning in the Netherlands

Patrick Witte and
Thomas Hartmann

R Routledge
Taylor & Francis Group

NEW YORK AND LONDON

First published 2022
by Routledge
605 Third Avenue, New York, NY 10158

and by Routledge
4 Park Square, Milton Park, Abingdon, Oxon, OX14 4RN

Routledge is an imprint of the Taylor & Francis Group, an informa business

Library of Congress Cataloging-in-Publication Data
Names: Witte, Patrick, author. | Hartmann, Thomas,
     1979– author.
Title: An introduction to spatial planning in the Netherlands /
     Patrick Witte and Thomas Hartmann.
Description: New York, NY : Routledge, 2022. | Includes
     bibliographical references and index.
Identifiers: LCCN 2021056273 (print) | LCCN 2021056274
     (ebook) | ISBN 9781032136981 (hardback) | ISBN
     9781032136998 (paperback) | ISBN 9781003230489 (ebook)
Subjects: LCSH: Land use—Netherlands—Planning. | Urban
     policy—Netherlands | Land use—Environmental aspects—
     Netherlands. | Sustainable architecture—Netherlands.
Classification: LCC HD108.6 .W58 2022 (print) | LCC
     HD108.6 (ebook) | DDC 333.73/1309492—dc23/
     eng/20211206
LC record available at https://lccn.loc.gov/2021056273
LC ebook record available at https://lccn.loc.gov/2021056274

ISBN: 978-1-032-13698-1 (hbk)
ISBN: 978-1-032-13699-8 (pbk)
ISBN: 978-1-003-23048-9 (ebk)

DOI: 10.4324/9781003230489

Typeset in Sabon
by Apex CoVantage, LLC

Planning education involves the scientific study of and training in creative conceptual and practical thinking on the relation between society and environment at various territorial levels and in the search, development and advancement of opportunities for purposeful intervention in that relation to ensure sustainable development.

Association of European Schools of Planning (AESOP), core requirements for a high-quality European Planning Education

Contents

Foreword: equality of parties   xi
Foreword: balancing planning practice and academia   xiv
Acknowledgement   xvi

1   Spatial planning – an exploration of the discipline   1
   1.1 Finding spatial planning – an approach to a
      definition 4
      1.1.1 Spatial planning and
          the future 5
      1.1.2 Spatial planning is comprehensive, not
          sectoral 9
      1.1.3 Planning as a public activity – the trias
          politica 11
   1.2 Spatial planning as a discipline – between
      practical application and an academic
      discipline 14
   1.3 The planning triangle 16
      1.3.1 Object 17
      1.3.2 Process 18
      1.3.3 Context 19
   1.4 Evolution of planning and its theory 21
      1.4.1 Focusing on the object: blueprint planning
          until the 1970s 21
      1.4.2 Focus on planning processes: collaborative
          planning around the 1990s 22
      1.4.3 Context matters at the start of the
          21st century 23

1.5 *Theory in practice – examples from the Netherlands 24*
   1.5.1 *Towards spatial planning as a national policy interest 24*
   1.5.2 *'The Dutch created the Netherlands' (1965–1985) 26*
   1.5.3 *'The Dutch Planner's Paradise' (1985–2010) 28*
   1.5.4 *'Paradise Lost?'—New challenges, and a new Act? (2010-present) 31*
1.6 *Conclusion: Entangled theory and practice 34*

2 **The object of planning: land-use**   36
2.1 *The object of planning: five key characteristics 36*
   2.1.1 *The physical connection of an object to a location (1) 37*
   2.1.2 *The inert nature of the object (2) 38*
   2.1.3 *The heterogeneity of the object (3) 38*
   2.1.4 *The functional possibilities of the object (4) 39*
   2.1.5 *The price of the object (5) 39*
2.2 *Spatial planning and land-use planning 40*
   2.2.1 *Different perspectives on the development of land-use 41*
   2.2.2 *The complexity of land-use 43*
2.3 *Land-use planning at different spatial scales 44*
   2.3.1 *National level 45*
   2.3.2 *Regional level 46*
   2.3.3 *Local level 46*
   2.3.4 *Multi-level dynamics 47*
2.4 *Land-use and scale: planning large-scale infrastructures 48*
   2.4.1 *Investing in large-scale infrastructure development 48*
   2.4.2 *The structuring effects of infrastructure: space and time 49*
   2.4.3 *Dutch example: the Betuweroute and the German hinterland 51*

2.5 *Discussion: scale and scarcity in Dutch land-use
planning 53*
2.6 *Conclusion: increasing normativity 54*

3 The process of planning: policy and governance   56
3.1 *The process of planning as a policy cycle 57*
   3.1.1 *Different phases of the planning process 57*
3.2 *Actors and governance – towards open planning
   processes 64*
   3.2.1 *Actors interact in governance networks 64*
   3.2.2 *Changing role of governance 65*
   3.2.3 *Governance and integrated planning 67*
3.3 *Example: Dutch regional governance 70*
   3.3.1 *Introducing the institutional void 70*
   3.3.2 *Complex regional planning challenges in
      the Netherlands 71*
   3.3.3 *Dutch provinces in regional governance:
      learning by doing 72*
3.4 *Discussion: the role of the planner in a
   governance setting 73*
3.5 *Conclusion: increasing normativity 75*

4 The context of planning: an administrative and
   institutional context   77
4.1 *The administrative context of planning 78*
   4.1.1 *Allocation and equivalence: the third
      aspiration level of Goedhart 78*
   4.1.2 *Financial flows and the principle of
      subsidiarity 81*
   4.1.3 *Dutch example: allocation issues and
      regional policy 82*
4.2 *The institutional setting of planning: the formal
   planning system 84*
   4.2.1 *Functions and tensions of the planning
      system 84*
   4.2.2 *Balancing tensions in planning 85*
   4.2.3 *Dynamics and performance of planning 89*

    *4.3 Discussion: societal developments and uncertain
       and complex planning challenges 92*
    4.4 Conclusion: increasing uncertainty 96

5   **Discussion: the planning triangle 'revisited'**   99
    5.1 Defined or open 99
        5.1.1 Defined and open objects of planning 100
        *5.1.2 Defined and open processes of
            planning 101*
        5.1.3 Defined and open contexts of planning 102
        *5.1.4 Dynamics of object, process, and
            context 103*
    *5.2 The 'Utrecht school': evolution of planning
       education and research 104*
    5.3 Epilogue by the authors 107

References   109
Index   124

Foreword
Equality of parties

It has been almost 30 years since I enjoyed great teaching from a famous American scholar. Professor Larry Susskind of the Massachusetts Institute of Technology gave a workshop on 'mediation' in the Netherlands, and I was lucky enough to be in the class. The fact that I was a planner in the tradition that I here refer to as the 'Utrecht School', resulted in the two of us immediately understanding each other in terms of content. Professor Susskind then concluded that the theme he had developed, namely mediation in spatial planning, was better suited to the Netherlands than to his own home country, the United States. To summarize: in his view, the citizen is not an opponent of the (planning) government, but the citizen can add value in the realization of governmental spatial plans. So, in his view on mediation, both parties are equal.

As a student, in 1963, I was writing a thesis about the area to the east of Apeldoorn – a medium-sized city in the Netherlands. I made my plan without consulting anyone. I had interviewed a lot of people, but I decided what was best! In our society this is approached quite differently now, of course. Lately, I have been thinking a lot about Susskind's view on the role of the citizen in spatial plans, and I have noticed that, even in contemporary spatial plans, the urban planner hired by the municipality sometimes still performs as I did in 1963. For instance, a residential complex for the disabled is being demolished near my house, and the municipality has been wanting to build a new housing area there. The residents of the neighbourhood came to the information evening, and everything seemed fine. A working group had been formed including a lawyer, an engineer, an architect, an economic geographer and the undersigned. The project further had the support of an additional 25 households. We made an alternative plan, and the city council then unanimously adopted our alternative. However, the town planner thought that he was the one who could do everything better and that he could and would arrange it all. The hired planner (from a consulting firm) tried to keep the citizens out of the process, and the municipal officers (plus the alderman) turned out not to be aware of their own policy.

My experience was once again that 'the planner' has the idea that he (or she) can arrange it much better by himself. He has studied for it, has experience, and therefore knows it much better. The citizen's participation only leads to delays and lowers the quality of the product. This is in stark contrast to the Utrecht School of spatial planning, that assumes that you cannot immediately apply the same story elsewhere. I think that mistake has been made often. In the early 1990s, for example, whole groups of planning professionals from Asia came to the Netherlands to see how we did planning in the Netherlands – but of course the principles aren't just immediately transferrable. Adaptation to a changing society is the first clear characteristic of the Utrecht planning heritage.

In order to give all people a fair chance in spatial planning processes (even with less expert stakeholders), help must also be offered to weaker parties. For example, in a case in Castricum – a small coastal town in the Netherlands – we created a few clear scenarios based on comparable cases. This allowed the citizen participants to better form their own judgement. It is precisely when the various parties can make an equal contribution to the process, that a good plan can be realized. For example, in an informal planning process, I once 'forced' the proponents to name all the negative aspects and let the opponents mention the benefits. This was necessary because the proponents were much more acquainted with the background of the situation than the opponents. Thus, a strong emphasis on process is crucial. I see this as a second characteristic of the Utrecht school of planning.

A third point for me is (still) the idea that you should look as far into the future as possible and then project your decision, your plan, into that future perspective. At a housing corporation where I once was a supervisory director, this meant that, instead of building more and more single-family homes, we started thinking about housing for the elderly and moving on. The houses had to last for more than 50 years! Related to this, I see a strong emphasis on spatial visions and the use of scenarios. So, a few elements are very typical: 1) citizens must be included in the process in a positive way; 2) the process is of the utmost importance and 3) you should look as far into the future as possible (supported by visions and scenarios).

Looking at teaching, we must acknowledge that most of our students end up in spatial planning practice. There they must use their scientific foundation. However, applying their academic knowledge in real life is a step that must absolutely be practised within the study programme itself. And that is why in Utrecht the 'planning studio' module was conceived as far back as 1996. In my opinion, this is an essential part because of another very important didactic aspect: the planning studio exercise is very motivating for many students. Utrecht students are well-received in practice for their skills in terms of cooperation. Team formation, division of tasks, mutual control: how do you teach students that? We already had the students form teams in the first month of the first year to jointly put down a product. While everyone knows that the planner must be ideally suited to work in a team, it is not a scientific characteristic, but it is an essential aspect of the training in Utrecht.

I have the impression that Dutch planning still belongs to the top planning countries in the world. And I think that our vision can be very inspiring for other countries. It was only when I worked at Utrecht University for a few years and went to an AESOP conference that I understood how Utrecht stood internationally: as a leader. My conclusion: the Utrecht professors Ton Kreukels and Tejo Spit had interpreted the profession of spatial planning in a way that was highly respected internationally. Spatial planning in Utrecht has maintained that position to date, and I hope it will remain so. It is precisely this wonderful harmony between science and society that remains so unique to the Utrecht vision. I therefore happily support the publication of this book. This is not about honour, but purely from the conviction that we can add something worthwhile to international spatial planning.

Dr. ir. Paul Zoete
Malden, July 16, 2019

Foreword
Balancing planning practice and academia

More than 20 years ago, Paul Zoete and I joined forces to write an introduction to urban and regional planning for Dutch planning students, based on our joint experience in spatial planning in the Netherlands. Together we shared decades of experience on all levels of government, but especially on the local and national level. Yet, at the same time, this book had to fulfil all academic requirements as well. To be honest, we struggled a lot with this mixed ambition. In order to structure a way out of this dilemma, we used the AESOP criteria (AESOP criteria, ECTP 2002) as a framework (on knowledge, competences, and attitudes) and filled it with our experiences in planning practice and planning research. In hindsight, the first editions of this introduction to spatial planning fully showed our concern for being too practical: next to the rather abstract reflections on our practical experiences, the first editions were also written rather compactly. These shortcomings were corrected in the later updates and, with the help of Annelies Beek, we considered the last edition (2016) to be rather balanced in this respect.

Now, Thomas Hartmann and Patrick Witte have taken this project one step further. Based on our original ambition, they broadened the scope of this introduction to spatial planning to an international scale. Therewith, they managed to make the original material, based on Dutch planning practice, accessible for an international public. Both Paul Zoete and I welcomed and supported this initiative, although we knew from experience what an exhausting exploration this would be. This included not only a mere translation, but also an update, a change of perspective and finding a new balance between the emphasis on planning and academic literature. It goes without saying that both Paul and I are proud of this first result, and we congratulate the authors on this first achievement. At the same time, we hope that this 'baby' will grow up, and that in the upcoming years, many more editions of this volume will be published.

Prof. dr. Tejo Spit
Utrecht, October 11, 2021

Acknowledgement

The Dutch approach of spatial planning and spatial development has influenced many countries in Europe and abroad. Since the Netherlands is a relatively small country with a dense population and scare land resources, smart acting and proper decision making in the field of spatial development are essential.

Especially the Utrecht School of Spatial Planning is well known for its innovative impulses in the triangle of object-, process-, and context-orientation. Patrick Witte and Thomas Hartmann, both with experience in teaching and researching at Utrecht University, demonstrate a precise overview in their handbook and give deep insights into the Dutch way of spatial planning and spatial development.

Prof. em. Dr. Bernd Scholl, ETH Zürich (Switzerland)

1 Spatial planning – an exploration of the discipline

This book discusses the **relation between spatial planning and spatial development**. It explores the academic underpinnings of the discipline and its practical implications, making use of insights on planning practices from the Netherlands. It develops an analytical framework to better carve out the cornerstones of the discipline and academic basis of spatial planning. This framework helps to systematize and address an 'implementation gap' in planning, in other words, this framework seeks to bridge the strategic and conceptual elements of spatial planning with its practical realization and implementation. The object, process, and context of planning and its interrelations are thoroughly discussed. In this introduction chapter, the central concepts and terms are introduced that will be discussed in detail throughout the following chapters of this book.

Throughout this book, reference is made to **Dutch spatial planning**, though many of the discussed aspects are relevant outside of this geographical and institutional context as well. The Netherlands is one of the most densely planned and populated countries in Europe, with spatial planning being deeply rooted in the Dutch culture of order and effect (Dekker *et al.* 2012). Although the Netherlands is a relatively small country, Dutch spatial planning is widely noticed and admired in the international literature (e.g., Faludi 1994; Wesselink *et al.* 2007; Schreuder 2001; Buitelaar 2010). The extensive references to the context of the Netherlands are in part due to the origin of this volume, as it builds on an earlier version published in Dutch, *Planologie – Een wetenschappelijke introductie in de ruimtelijke ordening in Nederland* (Spit and Zoete 2016), which has served as a basic introduction for students. But also, in a wider sense, the Netherlands provides a very suitable entrance point to understanding the basic rationales of planning. For example, in *Dutch Land-use Planning*, Needham deals with the land policy functions and effects of Dutch planning (Needham

DOI: 10.4324/9781003230489-1

2007). Also, in *Strong Stories – How the Dutch Are Reinventing Spatial Planning*, Hajer *et al.* (2010) reflect on planning-theoretical concepts in the Netherlands based on practical examples. This revised and rewritten version of the Dutch predecessor of this volume by Spit and Zoete (2016) is taking the Dutch planning system as a starting point and illustration to explain the basic functions and mechanisms of spatial planning. In doing so, it also positions itself in a broader international and academic debate on spatial planning as a discipline, in which the Netherlands is a much referred to context.

With this orientation, this book **complements other publications on spatial planning** as a discipline. For instance, Needham *et al.* (2018) explore the relation between planning, law, and economics. They focus foremost on land policy and provide reflections and theoretical considerations on planning and property, while this book discusses spatial planning more broadly as a discipline and illustrates this in an explorative way with practical examples from Dutch planning practice. This serves as an introduction to explain the functions and mechanisms of spatial planning. For more specific and in-depth information on the Dutch planning system, Needham's comprehensive book *Dutch Land-use Planning* (2014) explains in detail the Dutch planning system and land policy. Other examples are Van Dijk *et al.* (2019), who explain how distinct planning cultures can be identified across space and time within the Dutch planning system, and Dekker *et al.* (2012) who take a cultural-historical perspective on Dutch spatial planning.

One of the most iconic volumes for understanding Dutch planning is without a doubt Faludi and Van der Valk's 1994 publication on the Dutch planning doctrine in the 20th century. This is an important book – not least because it explains why and how the Netherlands have been considered a 'Planners' Paradise'. Zonneveld and Evers (2014) indeed praise the pedigree of Dutch planning as "an almost perfect example of a comprehensive integrated approach towards spatial planning" until the 1990s (p. 61). Moreover, Needham (2014) characterizes the past 30 years of Dutch planning as effective due to its proactive "planning by projects" (p. 220). In other words, Dutch planning is admired, but at the same time not static. This book tries less to evaluate and assess Dutch planning practice as such, but it provides – with practical examples from the Netherlands as one of the countries with a strong history in planning – **a framework to enable a structured reflection and discussion** of spatial planning.

This book builds on the **planning triangle** when exploring the basis of spatial planning in five main chapters.

The main function of the first chapter is to introduce the planning triangle. The planning triangle is an analytical framework that provides orientation in the discussion of different aspects of spatial planning, namely by distinguishing the **object, process, and context** of planning. These three dimensions function as a general structure for the remaining chapters in the book, to provide a comprehensive overview of the discipline. In addition, this introduction chapter presents a definition of spatial planning and relates planning to other disciplines. The struggle of spatial planning to be recognized as an academic discipline on the one hand and the need to link to practice on the other hand is explained.

The chapter then shows how spatial planning has changed and persisted over its short lifespan to date as an academic discipline. This development is linked to the development of planning theory. It is merely meant to provide an explorative orientation, not an attempt to comprehensively summarize the complexity of planning theory. The planning triangle serves to understand and interpret the different planning theoretical phases. With examples from Dutch planning – as a representation of what happened in Europe in these different phases – it is shown how **planning theory and practice** are intertwined and mirror each other.

The following three chapters each address one dimension of the planning triangle, whereas Chapter 2 focuses on the object of planning, Chapter 3 discusses the process of planning, and Chapter 4 focuses on the context of planning.

Chapter 2 on the **object of planning** focuses first on what it is that is planned. This chapter dives more deeply into key characteristics of the object of planning. A cornerstone of this chapter is to explain the basics of land-use planning in relation to different spatial scales. The chapter is illustrated with examples from Dutch spatial planning, such as strategic planning of large-scale infrastructure projects, with the general notions being applicable elsewhere (of course, embedded in different contexts and involving different processes). The examples thus help to understand the relation of the planning object with the process and context of planning, as we will see in the subsequent chapters.

Chapter 3 shines the spotlight on the **process of planning** and discusses the question of how something is planned, an issue of governance. Therefore, the definition of governance is addressed as well as the role of actors (i.e., stakeholders) within governance processes, and the relation between governance and integrated planning. With examples from regional governance, the chapter provides a useful toolbox for a deeper understanding and discussion of governance in and of planning.

Chapter 4 is dedicated to the **context of planning**. First, the planning context is described from a narrower perspective, namely the institutional system in which planning takes place. Second, the broader perspective is described, where planning is a mirror of external developments to planning, such as socio-economic changes, demographics, climate change, crises, etc. It is discussed how planning is always context specific and needs to be understood in its respective socio-spatial context. This elaboration on the context functions as a further elaboration and integration of the previous chapters to understand how the object of planning (i.e., 'what is planned') and the process of planning (i.e., 'how it is planned') take shape.

Ultimately, the book ends in Chapter 5 with **reflections on how the planning triangle may be useful** to close the gap between the conceptual elements of spatial planning and its practical realization. The concluding chapter brings together the three dimensions of the planning triangle and discusses how the planning triangle as an analytical tool can be used to position planning practice and research. It therefore reflects on planning practice, research, and education from the perspective and experience of the planning tradition developed at the faculty of Geosciences of Utrecht University in the Netherlands.

1.1 Finding spatial planning – an approach to a definition

What is spatial planning? Planning theorists affirm that there is not one generally accepted definition of spatial planning (Gunder and Hillier 2010). It is worth mentioning that spatial planning is not the same as land-use planning or zoning (the first being the European term, whereas zoning is used in the US context). Spatial planning is more comprehensive in terms of "subjects matter, territorial coverage, time-horizon and implementation tools" (Sclar *et al.* 2020, p. xix). There are many characterizations, for example, the EU Compendium of Spatial Planning Systems and Policies distinguishes four types of planning traditions: regional-economic, urbanism, comprehensive/integrated, and land-use planning (Shaw *et al.* 1995). Each of these types defines planning with different notions. In all planning traditions, however, planning can be considered as an intervention by a **public** authority (i.e., planning agency) to influence the **future** allocation and distribution of activities in **space** (Shaw *et al.* 1995), whereas the scale and scope of such interventions as well as the publicness of the intervention can differ. Nonetheless, three elements seem to be crucial for an understanding of planning: **public activity, future,** and **space** (in a wider or narrower sense) (Hillier 2010). So, in the following three sections, these three elements shall be discussed, starting with planning and the future (Section 1.1.1), followed by the role of space in planning (Section 1.1.2), and planning as a public activity (Section 1.1.3).

1.1.1 Spatial planning and the future

Planning is a long-term and open-ended exercise (Sclar *et al.* 2020, p. xix). Acting in the present, such as implementing spatial plans, influences what the space will look like in the future. When it comes to putting current action into a future perspective, it is therefore very important to have an idea of the desired future. That future – certainly in the longer term – is not predictable (it consists of past, present, and future elements), but it is conceivable (through projective or prospective future scenarios). As a result, spatial planning is also inextricably linked with uncertainties and ways to deal with uncertainties. The further away the planning horizon, the greater the uncertainty. This is nicely captured in a quote by the philosopher Francis Bacon: "They are ill discoverers that think there is no land, when they can see nothing but sea" (Kiernan, ed. 2000).

One of the tensions that are encountered, in particular – but not only – in binding land-use planning, is the tension between **inevitable uncertainties and necessary certainty.** Certainty is necessary, because planning provides social and economic stability by securing certain reliable property and development rights on land. Without certainty, many societal processes are hampered or are impossible – such as obtaining mortgages for housing, infrastructure investments, etc. This has to do with the long-term character of most land-uses – see also Needham *et al.* (2018) and Chapter 2. Such a perspective on certainty contrasts with strategic ambiguity in planning. **Strategic ambiguity** encourages flexibility in allowing different and contrasting interpretations to coexist, so that change and adaptation is possible to develop over time. In other words, it "leaves room for organizations to deny certain interpretations of their policies, permitting them to preserve future options" (Sohn and Edwards 2018, p. 553). So, there is a tension between certainty and flexibility in planning (Van den Hoek *et al.* 2020). This is also further discussed in Chapter 4.

To deal with this tension, spatial planning needs to **reduce uncertainties** and make them manageable. All kinds of methods and techniques are available to help the planner with this – such as planning-support systems (Geertman 2006), scenario approaches (Couclelis 2005), or futuring techniques (Hajer and Pelzer 2018). Depending on the type of spatial issue, its complexity and the duration of the process, a combination of methods can be employed to tackle the issues at hand. While this book touches upon some **planning methods**, it is not within the scope of this volume to explain these methods in detail.

A common method in planning are scenarios. In this, a distinction can be made between *projective* and *prospective* scenarios of dealing with the future (Hyatt *et al.* 1999). Projective scenarios use a technique called **forecasting** (De Haes 1995; Van der Steen 2017). Projective scenarios are based on the past and present, with the realization that the available data are, in principle, from the recent past. A time lag of a few months to two years is not uncommon. Planning therefore takes place on the 'facts of yesterday'. Such scenarios acknowledge that the near future can hardly be influenced, due to path dependencies. A very clear example of this was the imploding of the Dutch real estate market in 2010 two years after the collapse of Lehman Brothers and the global financial crisis in 2008; the **time lag effect** ('pipeline') ensured that spatial projects continued for two more years (Buitelaar and Witte 2011). However, spatial planning mostly works in the medium and long term (5 to 15 years, or longer). Based on analyses of developments and by calculations, a future vision can be sketched projectively for a distant moment 'on the horizon', followed by an extrapolation of potential developments. Projective scenarios are therefore often more conservative and realistic than prospective, which will be discussed next.

Prospective scenarios, in contrast, are drawn up with a completely different goal. They start with a vision based on the desirability of a certain long-term spatial outcome, and derive the steps to reach this vision. This is called **backcasting**. These prospective scenarios are often normative images that are based on certain values, norms, and belief-systems, for example, emerging or changing opinions about the importance of the environment, climate change, or healthy cities. An illustration of this is the changing notion of Dutch municipalities and their policies on the sustainability concept (Vroom and Van Straalen 2016). These visions of a desirable future then place current action in a future perspective and even attempt to steer spatial developments in the shorter term. Prospective scenarios usually forecast farther into the future than projective scenarios. A time span of 30 years is not considered unusual; sometimes planners even look 50 to 80 years ahead. For instance, spatial development visions for the Netherlands are currently sketched that envision the Netherlands in the year 2100 and beyond.

Both types of scenario methods are **normative** – but in different ways. While projective scenarios can be manipulated by including different data, prospective scenarios can be much more progressive in their normative character. A classic but still relevant example from infrastructure planning concerns the statistics on expected growth in car ownership in a certain area. One way to develop a scenario based on this growth is that new roads and infrastructure are necessary to facilitate the growth – upgrading and widening of existing roads, expansion of parking facilities in public spaces, etc. An alternative prospective scenario can be to derive the idea that public transport facilities and other non-polluting ways of transport need to be improved, for example, by a higher frequency of trains, more comfort, and higher reliability. This is especially relevant in the light of current discussions on the potential post-fossil or post-car future of cities and the increased emphasis on sustainable mobility alternatives, such as electric vehicles or (smart) shared mobility concepts.

Such **normativity in scenarios** applies to all issues in spatial planning – housing shortage can be interpreted as a need to develop more housing or a need to influence the demand of housing; increasing flood risk in urban areas can call for higher dikes or for better adaptation, etc. The question which direction is preferable, and which not is thus a normative one, and it is increasingly influenced by a growing pluralism in society in which other stakeholders besides the government increasingly have their voices heard (e.g., Snel *et al.* 2019 on pluralism in flood risk management). Planning, in preparing and working towards realizing such scenarios, is thus inevitably normative. Planners need to be aware of this normativity (Section 1.1.3) and systematically think about realizing the desired futures.

Systematic thinking about the future is an inherent part of spatial planning to prepare proportionate interventions. The fact that the future entails many conceivable possibilities creates opportunities but also responsibilities for planners. Planning current interventions based on a future perspective is a very essential feature of planning as a public activity (Figure 1.1). One of the ways to put current action into a future perspective is to draw up a spatial plan. The future will be influenced with these spatial plans to the degree that these plans are binding for landowners and authorities in other sectors (Section 1.1.2).

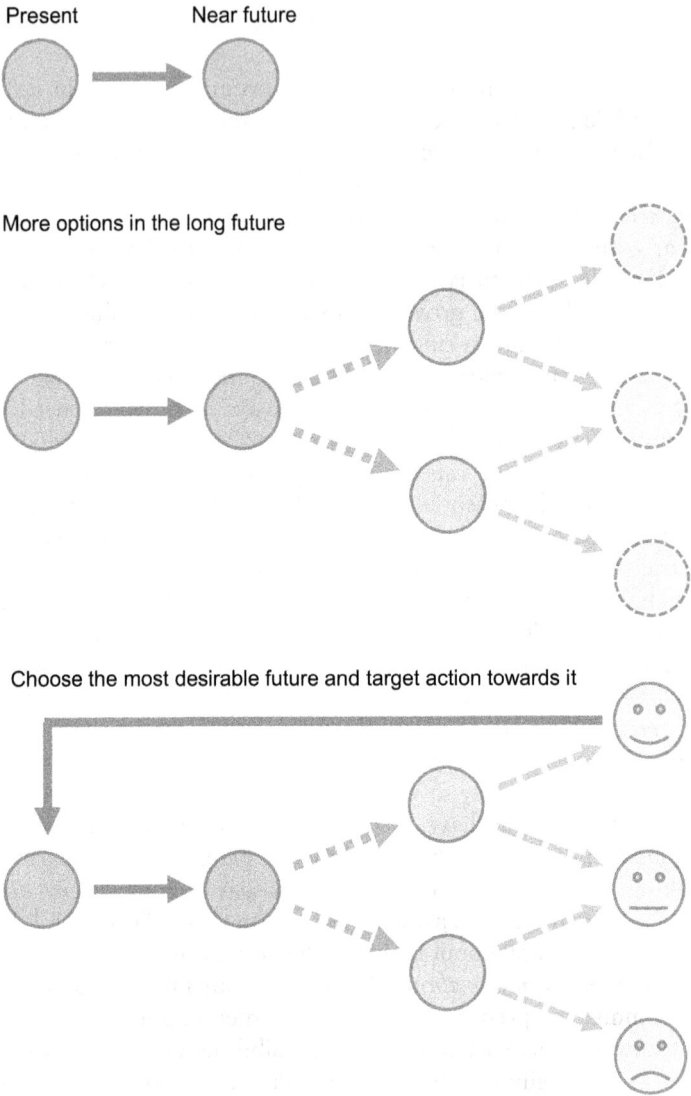

Present   Near future

More options in the long future

Choose the most desirable future and target action towards it

Figure 1.1 Using future visions to determine a course of current action

Public interest is an important factor in deciding on the desired future outcome, although public interest is an abstract concept to grasp, with many different and competing ways to define it (Alexander 2002). Beyond its different definitions, public interest is also dynamic and constantly changing. The priorities that are set for spatial policy are thus also exposed to these dynamics. The important question arises, to what extent (urban) areas can tackle the specific and upcoming problems of today and the challenges for the near future. Such problems and challenges can result from, for example, institutional, environmental, or socio-economic changes (Needham and Hartmann 2012). Institutional changes can be, for example, new supranational legislation or treaties or a changing political climate. Changing environmental conditions can result from climate change. The new requirements on healthy cities following the ongoing Corona crisis in 2020–2021 has presented such a societal challenge. Economic changes can result from economic crises such as the global economic collapse of 2008, which led to new dynamics of land markets and the rise of legal reforms. All such problems and challenges affect the public interest to which spatial planning is ultimately dedicated.

This implies that **planning is never 'finished'**. Society and its interests are constantly changing (such as the population, the numbers and types of housing, mobility, prosperity, and forms of recreation), which is why different claims are being made on the allocation and distribution of scarce spatial resources. And that is why spatial planning is never 'finished': adaptation to a changing society is constantly needed!

This means planning needs to continuously re-evaluate and adjust plans, while at the same time providing necessary legal certainty and ensure socio-economic functioning of cities. This is a difficult and always political balance to strike. **Balancing** in planning is difficult. Planning for the future requires a good understanding of the historical development as well as learning from the past to avoid repeating mistakes. This means that planners should not only look back at substantial and procedural choices made, but also at the contexts within which those choices were made (Figure 1.2).

1.1.2 Spatial planning is comprehensive, not sectoral

Space matters in spatial planning. The object of reference in planning is space, or rather a territory (e.g., a neighbourhood, municipality, region, or a state), in a comprehensive sense, not a topic or a sector. Spatial planning differs in this respect from sectoral planning (e.g., agriculture, tourism, transport, etc.).

Choose the most desirable future and target action towards it

Understand the past to
determine future paths

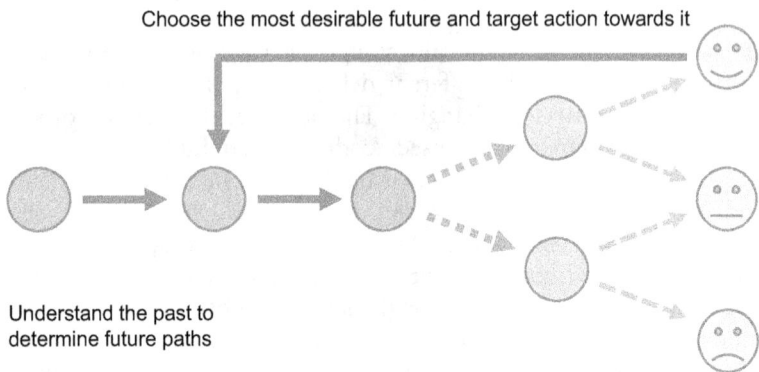

Figure 1.2 Planning for the future requires an understanding of the past

Sectoral planning involves the implementation of a specific policy of a branch of public services, aimed at the provision of those
services, such as transportation, water management, nature conservation, or agriculture. Often, such services at the national level
coincide with a department or a part thereof, for example the Min-
istry of Defense or Infrastructure Works (i.e., the Dutch *Rijkswater-
staat*). Spatial planning – in contrast – has the task to consider space
comprehensively and integrally (Vigar 2009). This means, spatial
planning must take all sectoral planning activities into consideration
and coordinate them. Figure 1.3 illustrates the difference between
sectoral and **comprehensive planning** (we refer in the remainder of
the book to spatial planning, implying that it is by definition a comprehensive activity).

The **distinction between sectoral and spatial planning** is partly a
historical and partly an analytical distinction. The distinction has
been especially of importance in the early days of spatial planning
as a discipline – when its main function indeed was the coordination
of all sectoral policies. This will be shown later in this chapter. However, sectoral planning is gradually and increasingly changing: firstly,
because sectoral planning becomes more integral and comprehensive –
such as water management (Hartmann and Spit 2015b) or transport
planning (Witte 2014), secondly, because spatial policies are increasingly intertwined and integrated – such as in the Environment and Spatial Planning Act (*Omgevingswet*). This makes the relation between

← COMPREHENSIVE PLANNING →

SPATIAL PLANNING

SECTORAL PLANNING ↗

Housing

Transport

Environment

Agriculture

Tourism

Industry

Energy

Water

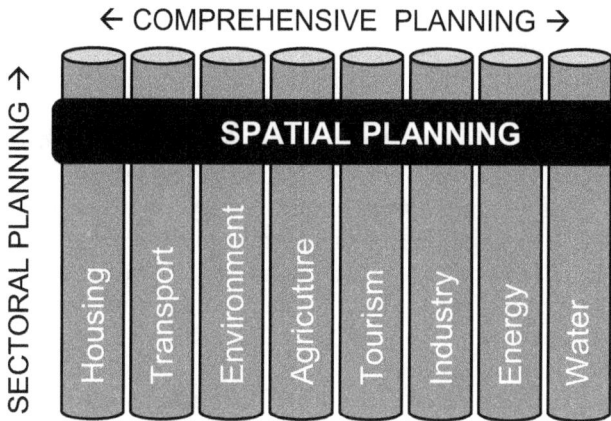

Figure 1.3 Spatial planning and sectoral planning

spatial planning and sectoral planning increasingly complex as more sectors are starting to develop their own spatial policies (Hartmann and Driessen 2017).

1.1.3 Planning as a public activity – the trias politica

Planning is a **public activity** that is concerned with spatial development. But next to spatial planning as a public activity, other sectors and private stakeholders, such as real estate investors, construction industry, architects, and even civil initiatives and citizens influence spatial development. So, is every activity that influences spatial development spatial planning? Such a view would undermine any definition of spatial planning – or as Wildavsky (1973) once put it: "If planning is everything, then maybe it is nothing". To distinguish planning from reactive interventions or short-term spatial activities, we conceive of spatial planning as an action of a public authority (Needham *et al.* 2018). Some approaches to spatial planning conceive of a much wider definition of spatial planning, such as the actor-relational approach (Boelens 2009) or informal planning and self-organization (Van Straalen *et al.* 2017). Narrowing planning down to a public activity excludes real estate development or guerrilla gardening from the definition (alternatively, they are considered as spatial developments). Second, spatial planning is a deliberately future-oriented activity (Hillier

2010). This means that spatial planning takes the distant future explicitly into account.

In agreement with the European compendium on spatial planning (Shaw *et al.* 1995), Voogd (1995) defines spatial planning as: *"the systematic preparation of policymaking and relevant actions for implementing policy, aimed at consciously intervening in the spatial development, including the organization of these interventions, in order to preserve and improve spatial quality"* (p. 5). The pursuit of maintaining or improving spatial quality is a normative goal. After all, what is an improvement for one person does not necessarily have the same meaning for others. In fact, spatial planning considerations often concern issues in which opposing interests must be weighed against each other, such as nature conservation versus infrastructure development. The valuation of the result of that assessment thus becomes dependent on one's perspective (Davy 1997). If it is also considered that judgements about spatial quality differ over time, it seems better to adjust this ambition over time. In our own definition of spatial planning we therefore align with Voogd, except for his emphasis on the ambition of spatial quality. The definition we use is broader and regards spatial planning much less as a linear process towards an ever better spatial quality: **the systematic preparation of policy-making and executive actions that are aimed at consciously intervening in spatial order and at organizing these interventions.**

This definition positions planning in different phases in the policy cycle at the same time. The **policy cycle** describes a heuristic model of public policy, which reiterates sequential steps of policy programming (i.e., problem recognition, proposal of a solution, and choice of a solution), policy implementation, and evaluation of the effects of a policy (Knoepfel *et al.* 2011). This is further explored in Chapter 3. Planning as 'preparing policy-making' refers to the influence of planning on the problem recognition and proposal of solutions. Planning can thus be conceived as policy programming by preparing spatial plans and visions that solve a specific spatial problem or nurture a desired spatial situation. Policy programming constitutes the "political definition of the public problem" (Knoepfel *et al.* 2011, p. 196). This entails that the problem definition – for example: affordability of housing is a matter of undersupply of housing units – is a result of a political-normative process. However, policymaking is just "prepared" by planning. The formal policy programming is left to the legislative branch of the state (Figure 1.4). This raises the question how planning is positioned within the state.

Legislative

Trias
Politica

Executive   Judicative

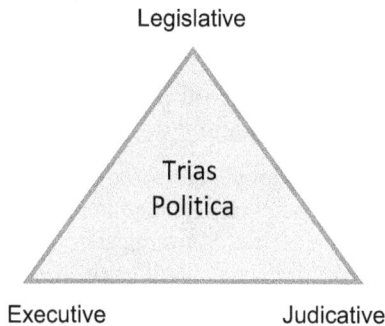

Figure 1.4 Trias Politica

An important pillar in liberal democracies is the separation of powers into three branches: the legislative, the executive, and the judicial branch. These three form the so-called *trias politica* (Figure 1.4). The trias politica prevents the abuse of power (Persson *et al.* 1997) by creating checks and balances between the three branches. These three branches exist on all levels of the state – meaning the national level, the regional (or provincial) and the municipal (local) level, even on the level of supranational bodies (such as the European Union).

The *legislative branch* consists of elected politicians who are responsible for making laws. On the national level, it is institutionalized in Parliament. On the local level, where binding land-use planning mostly takes place, it is embodied in the city councils. The *executive branch* implements and enforces the law. On the national level it is the government and its dedicated ministers (chosen by the political parties who form the coalition), at the municipal level it is the mayor and the aldermen (the aldermen are all members of the political parties that are forming the coalition together). The *judicial branch* consists of the courts and its organs. They intervene in the actions of executive bodies if laws are not followed properly, but they can also intervene if legislative bodies disregard higher principles such as constitutional law. Spatial planning belongs to the executive branch of the state. It is therefore expected to follow and implement the law as formulated by the legislature, and it is controlled by the judicial branch of the state. Planning implements law by using regulations. Needham (2007) puts this statement into question by stressing that the formal planning processes – at least in the Netherlands – often are at the end of a preparatory and often more informal planning process. This interpretation is also further explored within this book.

1.2   Spatial planning as a discipline – between practical application and an academic discipline

If planning is merely the implementation of public policy, is planning then its own academic discipline? Academic programs in spatial planning are rather young. The first planning school was founded in Liverpool, UK, in 1909. In the second half of the 19th century, the rapid growth of cities during the industrial revolution led to poor living conditions (Hartmann and Needham 2012; Hartmann and Geertman 2016; Needham 1988; Taylor 1998). Spatial planning emerged out of the recognition that different sectoral policies influence spatial development (e.g., policies on housing development, public space, infrastructure systems, etc.); hence, planning influences how land is used and how cities and regions function and are built. However, a comprehensive and overarching institution that brings together and balances the different sectoral ideas to ultimately govern urban development in the public interest was lacking. Such an institution was needed to connect different disciplines related to sectoral planning.

Unsurprisingly, planning is related to and overlaps with many other disciplines (Parker and Doak 2012), such as public administration and policy science, urban and economic geography, urban design and landscape architecture. Planning needs to position itself against these disciplines (Figure 1.5).

Planning is analytical. Planning has a substantial effect on peoples' daily lives. Planning influences how cities are shaped, how commuters come to work, how families live, and where facilities are. Planning also makes people poorer or richer by influencing property rights (Needham *et al.* 2018). Planning uses public power, money, and trust. This bears responsibility for the actors who oversee planning. Therefore, planning interventions ought to be based on a sound analysis of the spatial problem and its solutions. The spatial analysis component of spatial planning overlaps with geography – with all its sub-disciplines ranging from physical to economic or urban geography. Planners need to be familiar with methods and theories from geography or related disciplines in the social sciences. The emphasis on the spatial analysis of spatial situations distinguishes planning as a discipline from urban design or landscape architecture, which tend to be much more focused on conceptualizations and its realization, whereas the focus on the (distant) future distinguishes planning from geography.

	What is wrong?	What should be done?
in theory		
in practice		

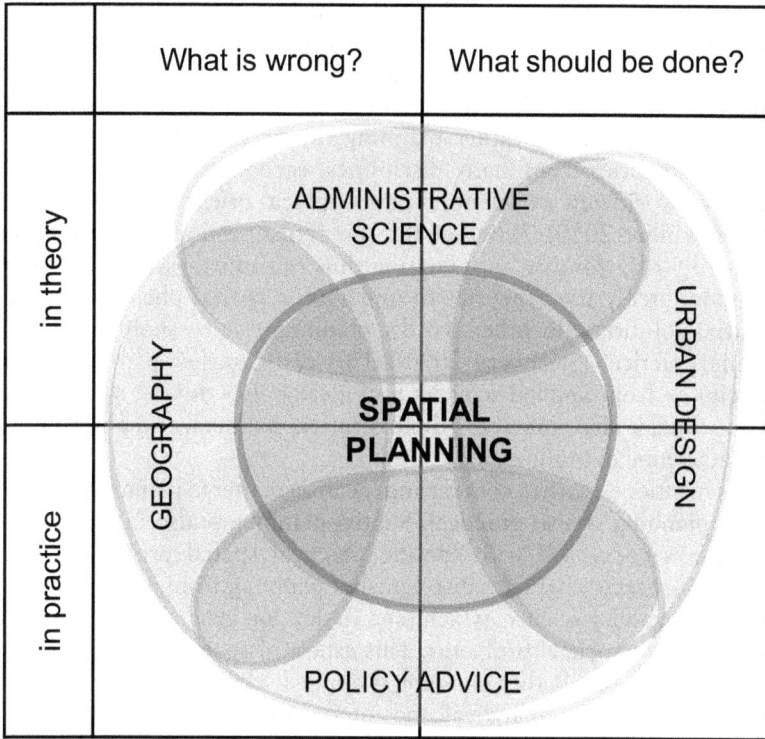

The table headers and axis labels read: "What is wrong?", "What should be done?", "in theory", "in practice", "ADMINISTRATIVE SCIENCE", "GEOGRAPHY", "SPATIAL PLANNING", "URBAN DESIGN", "POLICY ADVICE"

Figure 1.5 Spatial planning and other disciplines

Planning intervenes. While geography focuses on analyzing a spatial situation, spatial planning also aims at intervening in such situations with a future-oriented perspective. This is where planning and urban design and landscape architecture overlap. Planning education therefore should also always contain some sort of integrative project or studio work (Hengstermann and Hartmann 2021), as is, for example, the case in the curriculum of Utrecht University (Hartmann and Spit 2015c). In other words, spatial planning as a discipline does not only analyze what is happening but also suggests what should be done in a certain spatial situation.

Planning is also theoretical. Like planning, planning theory is still young. Still, planning theory must provide a scientific foundation for planning as a discipline (Hartmann and Geertman 2016).

Problem descriptions and interventions in space are reflected in planning with a broader set of theories. Planning theory is thereby not a confined body of theories, but it is a constantly evolving assembly and application of theories derived from other fields (Yiftachel and Huxley 2000). Planning theorists do not agree on an ultimate planning theory, but rather planning theory consists of a body of various theories from many disciplines, each stemming from a distinctive worldview or scientific-philosophical orientation (Needham 1988; Hillier 2010). Whether the theoretical notion of planning is a theory 'of', 'for', or 'in' planning thus remains up for debate, but it undoubtedly used theories to understand spatial phenomena and spatial solutions. In other words, planning theory should 'help to guide practice' (Sternberg 2000). This distinguishes planning as a discipline from applied sciences and mere policy advice, and, at the same time, it also embraces administrative, political, and philosophical academic disciplines.

As mentioned earlier, context and location matter in planning. Therefore, **planning is also practical.** Spatial planning – also in research – is always concerned with specific practical spatial problems. This location-specific character distinguishes planning from administrative science or policy science, which tend to develop general (i.e., isotopic) solutions for societal problems. This aspect of spatial planning opens the debate as to whether planning is applied science or not.

Planning is thus analytical and intervenes in space, and it is also theoretical and practical. In this respect, it bridges disciplines and is inter-disciplinary. This implies that finding and defining the identity of planning is a difficult endeavour. In the following section a framework is introduced to capture the essence and nature of spatial planning. We refer to this **framework** as the **planning triangle.**

1.3 The planning triangle

Spatial planning deals with the allocation and distribution of land and other spatial resources. Planners pursue this task by using governmental power, economic incentives, and communicative strategies. The activity of planning raises many questions and dilemmas with respect to efficiency, effectiveness, justice, legitimacy, and many more (Needham *et al.* 2018). It is important for spatial planners to reflect on their activity in a systematic and structured way. One way to gain more insight into this matter is to distinguish three dimensions that together structure the field of activity for the planner: the **object, process, and context of planning.**

Spatial planning problems can be approached from three different but interrelated angles (or dimensions) (Spit and Bertolini 1998; Spit and Zoete 2016; Driessen *et al.* 2012). The object relates to the content of a planning issue. This could be, for example, a question about housing, the allocation of public facilities, a mobility problem, or challenges in the interaction between space and water. The process is then understood as the interaction between actors and resources, especially how they are used to achieve specific planning objectives. The context refers to the institutional and societal conditions (or environmental variables) in which objectives regarding object and process can be realized. These can be societal or economic trends and developments, institutional developments such as changing laws, regulations, norms, and customs, but also changes or restrictions in the environment, such as economic or political developments (Hartmann and Spit 2015c). These three dimensions can be found in varying degrees in all planning activities. Depending on the issue and the ways in which those involved look at it, emphasis can be placed on object, process, or context. This means that **every spatial planning situation is unique!** In the following sections, we briefly touch upon each of these three core dimensions of the planning triangle.

1.3.1 Object

Planning decides on the allocation and distribution of land-uses by allowing or restricting how specific pieces of land may be used (Needham *et al.* 2018). The object of planning relates to the content of the respective planning issue, a specific allocation or distribution of land-uses. Formally, the object of spatial planning represents the way spatial resources are used, namely the land-use. This may be, for example, the realization of housing, the allocation of public facilities, but also certain mobility solutions (e.g., transit-oriented development solutions, mobility-as-a-service concepts), or changes in use or disposal rights of certain spatial goods such as restrictions for certain land-uses following a binding land-use plan (e.g., development-free zones due to restrictive noise or air pollution regulations). In other words, the object of planning is about the question: '**What is planned?**' The objects of national or regional planning are different from municipal land-use planning or sectoral planning, as will be shown in more detail in Chapter 4.

Dilemmas on the object of planning unfold around conflicts of land-use. Land-uses often can be in conflict with each other. Land that is designated as industrial area cannot be protected landscape at the same time; residential land cannot be combined with every other type of land-use, etc. As land is a scarce resource and this scarcity is partly a consequence of planning (Hartmann and Gerber 2018), planners are often confronted with deciding for the one and against other land-uses. This, by definition, entails planning dilemmas, as often multiple land-uses are possible and even desirable. Clear examples of planning dilemmas related to scarcity of land in the Netherlands are the preserving of open space in the Randstad metropolitan area through the Green Heart planning doctrine (Van der Valk and Faludi 1997) or mega-infrastructure development such as the extension of the Second Maasvlakte in the Port of Rotterdam or the development of the Betuweroute freight railway (e.g., Witte 2014; Teisman *et al.* 2009).

Theories concerning the planning object are for example allocation theories, such as Christaller's Central Place Theory or Von Thünen's Model of Agricultural Land Use. Such 'substantive' theories (Fainstein 2005) help to better understand the dilemmas at stake by quite pragmatically teaching how certain planning designations affect land markets – do they follow the economic development patterns or contradict them? Answers to such questions help to better design planning processes (Section 1.3.2). Not only land economics, such as land rent, but also concepts of sustainable or resilient land-uses can provide theoretical or conceptual lenses to understand dilemmas on the object or provide guidance in solving them (Gunder and Hillier 2010). Next to that, theories on behaviour are relevant to understanding the planning object better, such as the Tragedy of the Commons (Hardin 1968) or the Coase Theorem (1960). Hardin explains how certain types of goods, namely the commons, can be over-used without interventions, while Coase unpacks conditions that lead to an optimal allocation of goods based on markets. These two examples of theories illustrate how the object of planning is affected by the users, and they also hint at the relevance of planning interventions: namely to prevent inefficient use (Hardin) or intervene in distribution of costs and benefits (Coase). How planning interventions work is essentially also a question of the process.

1.3.2 Process

There are different ways how planning can exactly intervene in the allocation and distribution of land. These ways relate to the planning process. This is thus the question: '**How is it planned?**' This question entails both a formal and a pragmatic side. The formal side refers to the rules set out in planning law, such as certain mandatory steps in a policy cycle or planning process, including participation or stakeholder involvement. The Environment and Spatial Planning Act (*Omgevingswet*) also foresees participation as a mandatory step in land-use planning processes (Hartmann *et al.* 2018). The pragmatic side goes beyond this formal process and entails open and rather informal planning processes with early-stage drafts, scenario-thinking methods, or the implementation of planning with other (private or civil) stakeholders besides the government. So, the process dimension of planning focuses on the interaction between actors and resources, and how they contribute to achieving certain planning objectives.

Planning as a public activity ultimately needs to **balance different interests**. The design of the planning process is also inherently political and can involve power imbalances and diverging values between actors. It thus can exclude or include certain stakeholders, for example, by employing certain planning methods and planning instruments, but also time and scale of planning processes can have substantial impact on planning processes. Dilemmas that arise in planning processes can concern the relation between legitimacy, democracy, and effectiveness of planning processes. Making a process very open can seriously influence the efficiency of its progress, while closing the planning process can also have severe effects for the implementation, especially if resistance against planning projects jeopardizes the intended outcome. Determining whom to involve, how, and when requires a well-designed planning process.

Procedural planning theories can provide the necessary analytical and conceptual framework to design (or co-design) better planning processes. Such theories entail theories on collaboration and communication (Healey 2003; Yiftachel and Huxley 2000), governance (Driessen *et al.* 2012; Torfing and Ansell 2016), but also on formal planning processes. A lot of such theories originate from administrative and political science (Scharpf 1997; Gerber *et al.* 2009), such as theories on legitimacy or property rights (Bromley 1991). In this book, we will particularly relate to the ongoing academic debates on (urban) governance to illustrate academic reflections on the process of planning.

1.3.3 Context

Spatial planning is locationally specific. What works in location A does not necessarily work in location B. The context dimension of planning thus refers to the preconditions of the setting (or contextual variables) in which planning is realized (Gualini 2010). This can be in a wider sense related to societal trends and developments, but also in a narrower sense be mostly affected by changes or limitations in the institutional context, such as economic, juridical, administrative, or political developments.

The context can have a major impact on the **success or failure of planning**. If a commercial area is developed in an area of growth or shrinkage, in times of economic prosperity or in crisis, as part of a trend or outside of it, in a left-wing or a right-wing political climate, etc. – such aspects fundamentally matter in planning and are crucial to understanding a particular planning outcome. Policy is inherently reacting to societal developments. Though policy aims are to some extent also steering these developments, the democratic control of policy – sometimes very indirectly – requires policy also to react to societal developments. Spatial planning, in bringing different policy fields together and translating these policies into comprehensive planning, can thus be regarded as a *"mirror of societal developments"* (Kreukels 1985). Societal changes thus influence planning and trigger new spatial developments. Spatial planning is therefore not only locationally specific, but also 'a child of its time'. Planning, as shaping the future but being positioned in present times, therefore faces the dilemma if it is to merely react to or also to some extent shape planning contexts. The extent to which planners have an influence over societal developments through their planning interventions is therefore often debated. It goes without saying that planners themselves are oftentimes overoptimistic about the actual influence they have over shaping socio-spatial outcomes.

Theories relevant to understand planning **contexts** stem from different disciplines. Examples are transition theories (e.g., Frantzeskaki and De Haan 2009; Rotmans *et al.* 2001), concepts of path dependency, windows of opportunities, or lock-in situations (e.g., Boschma *et al.* 2017; Arthur 1989), but also cultural or political theories that help understanding planning contexts, such as Cultural Theory (Douglas 1986) or institutional theory (e.g., Monstadt 2007; North 1990). Such theories situate the respective planning problem within its specific circumstances. A very practical illustration of the influence of context on spatial planning outcomes in the Netherlands is the variety of municipal responses to the global economic collapse of 2008 in terms of their approaches towards land policy. After the economic crisis of 2008–2010, land policy is shifting more and more from either active or passive land policies towards so-called situational land policies, depending on the size and scope of the municipality, and the planning issue at stake (Van Oosten *et al.* 2018).

1.4 Evolution of planning and its theory

This section further elaborates upon the academic debates on spatial planning (i.e., planning theory): it explores how planning theory evolved along the analytical dimensions of the object, process, and context of planning. The subsequent section then illustrates these theoretical notions with practical examples from the historical development of planning in the Netherlands. This shows how **planning theory and practice are entangled** and can be better understood in relation to each other.

Just after World War II, spatial planning in Europe started to develop as an independent academic discipline. Accordingly, planning theory has evolved significantly during the short history of its existence. **Three main phases** can be distinguished: blueprint planning (1940s–1970s), collaborative planning (1980s–1990s), and open planning (2000s–2010s). These phases can be characterized as in the following sections.

1.4.1 Focusing on the object: blueprint planning until the 1970s

In the **post-war period from 1945 to the 1970s**, spatial planning was dominated by reconstruction. During the post-war period, planning had to resolve urgent and rather technical issues, such as rebuilding destroyed cities in Europe, constructing roads, infrastructure, and public spaces, and providing essential facilities; spatial problems appeared to be relatively easy: "definable, understandable and consensual" (Rittel and Webber 1973, p. 156). These tasks needed planners capable of realizing such tasks with great effectiveness and efficiency. Spatial planning was "essentially an exercise in **physical planning and design**" (Taylor 1998).

In this phase, comprehensive and general plans were made to realize them in an effective and efficient way. Such planning is called "**blueprint planning**", where spatial planners made informed decisions based on theories that helped to find the best land-uses for respective locations. Planning was analytical and conceptual, using theories from related academic fields such as transport planning, urban design, or economics to understand the object of planning (Needham 1988).

The planner presented in the plans a final vision of an area that was expected to be realized eventually. Steps in planning processes were chronological. Planners considered themselves **engineers of space** (Albers 1969; Allmendinger 2002).

1.4.2 Focus on planning processes: collaborative planning around the 1990s

However, the practice of spatial planning soon learned that a linear progression of such step-by-step schemes does not work. After all, in planning practice, it turned out that in one phase the next phase is anticipated, while in the next phase there is continuous feedback to the previous phases. Planning processes thus proceed much more iteratively than the phases as sketched in the previous sections would suggest. During the 1960s, this became increasingly apparent. Around the 1970s, a **major paradigm shift** took place in spatial planning. By then, city centres were restored, and urban life flourished. Citizens became assertive and claimed participation and active involvement in decision-making (Baum 1977). This was the time when Jane Jacobs objected to rational-comprehensive city planning in the USA (Jacobs 1961), students revolted against traditional systems and for more democracy (Selle 2010), and Arnstein advocated for participation to empower citizens (Arnstein 1969). Spatial planning as a 'mirror of society' (Kreukels 1985) adjusted to these trends, and it became increasingly complex, normative, and inherently uncertain (Hartmann 2012). Rittel and Webber (1973) coined the term "wicked problems" to describe these planning intricacies. The response was a new planning paradigm that focused much more on planning processes than solely on the object of planning.

The new paradigm that emerged represented a major disruption to the way planners approached problems. The fundamental change was indicated by the different names linked to the new paradigm: 'post-positivist', 'post-industrial', 'post-Fordist', or 'post-modern' planning (Healey 1996; Hendriks 1999; Alexander 2000; Allmendinger 2002). Despite the different notions of the term, the common idea of using these **post-isms** was the **rejection of object-oriented concepts** of earlier periods (Baum 1977; Allmendinger 2002; Hartmann and Geertman 2016; Allmendinger and Tewdwr-Jones 2002). According to this new understanding, planning problems and solutions need to be sought in a complex network of stakeholders and actors beyond rationalist reasoning.

Process planning thus made its appearance in spatial planning. Planning in this phase focused much more on the planning activity itself than on the content or object of planning. Different schools of thoughts entered the planning debate – inspired by Luhmann or Habermas. For Luhmann, communication is the way systems evolve and act. It is the distinction in code of communications that sets the subsystems apart. Luhmann's vision was that problems are solved through conflict between systems via communication (Kihlström 2012). Habermas agrees that communicative action leads to problem-solving, but he assumes that communication inherently contains the possibility of consensus (Huxley 2000). Both schools of thought are very different, but they have in common that both emphasize the role of **communication in problem solving**.

Communicative planning (Huxley 2000; Healey 1996) and participatory planning (Innes and Booher 2000) were born. In this vein, collaboration, participation, and citizen initiatives were celebrated in planning theory as the panacea for wicked planning problems (Hajer *et al.* 2010; Klemme and Selle 2010; Fagence 1977; Brownill and Carpenter 2007; Dreijerink *et al.* 2008). The most dominant term in this time was '**collaborative planning**', brought to the debate by Healey (1997). The label has been used and misused since its introduction for all sorts of inclusive and participative governance processes in spatial planning (Healey 2003).

One form of process-oriented planning was the **strategic choice approach** (Friend and Jessop 2013). An important merit of the strategic choice approach was that it showed in a systematic way that complex planning processes could indeed be structured, including feedback cycles (Diller and Oberding 2017). With the introduction of the strategic choice approach, the process element can no longer be ignored, whether in the practice of planning in academia or its real-life practice. At the same time, this approach was not insensitive to signals from the context of planning development: its surrounding society.

1.4.3 Context matters at the start of the 21st century

The strong **process-orientation in planning** has been **criticized** since the turn of the 21st century. Gradually, the awareness prevailed that planning and planning processes do not take place in a vacuum. Such processes are influenced by the contexts in which they take place. Critique of mainly process-oriented planning stems from within spatial planning and theory itself (Needham and Hartmann 2012; Fainstein 2005; Gunder and Hillier 2010), but also more broadly from a neo-institutionalist perspective, which tries to understand institutions in a wider context of social interactions (Debrunner and Hartmann 2020; Dembski and Salet 2010). The notion was that "a narrow definition of planning theory results in theoretical weakness arising from the isolation of process from context and object" (Fainstein 2005, p. 121). Planning theorists were starting to search for a more general theory of planning (Gunder and Hillier 2010; Gunder *et al.* 2018). Such a theory should not only help to make better plans (Forester 2004) but should also help spatial planning to address the grand issues – climate change, energy and mobility transitions, demographic change, socio-economic dynamics, digitalization, or global pandemics.

This recent development in planning theory marks a shift in which the broader context of planning becomes increasingly important. Planning in such theoretical notions understands itself beyond the mere production of housing or provision of planning procedures to facilitate decisions on land-use. Rather, spatial planning since the turn of the 21st century understands itself as **pro-actively shaping and co-creating society.** This, of course, raises many issues regarding effectiveness, efficiency, justice, and legitimacy of planning.

1.5 Theory in practice – examples from the Netherlands

The evolution of Dutch planning also shows how different emphasis on parts of the planning triangle (object, process, context) is practically visible in materialized space over the course of time. The phases as described in the previous section were less linear in practice than depicted here. Still, some practical illustrations can be seen in looking at concrete examples of Dutch land-use planning. Also, the phases are not sequential, as the order of the earlier sections might suggest, but they are rather complementary. With **showcases from the Netherlands,** this section shall illustrate how trends in planning theory can be recognized in the built environment, with attention to object-centred, process-focused, and context-oriented planning developments. Along with this, attention is also afforded to how developments in the theory are reflected in Dutch national policies on spatial planning. The materialization of these policies can be clearly seen in the showcases of residential developments in and around the city of Utrecht (Nieuwegein, Leidsche Rijn, and the Merwedekanaalzone). The cases thereby show almost ideal-typical situations, which might not be found everywhere in spatial developments of the respective periods.

1.5.1 *Towards spatial planning as a national policy interest*

A sound understanding of the policy history of Dutch spatial planning is crucial in order to avoid making the same mistakes over again, but also to understand the context in which certain choices were made.

Furthermore, in making predictions and creating scenarios for the future, it is crucial to also understand the 'past and present elements of the future' through a brief overview of the policy history of planning in the Netherlands. We will not go into detail on the very early history of Dutch spatial planning, as this has been extensively covered in De Klerk and Van der Wouden (2021). Rather, we briefly highlight some key moments of the period up to 1965 – the moment in time when the first planning act was installed in the Netherlands (WRO/Bro). We then move on to discuss some key developments in planning theory in the national memoranda on spatial planning, linked to the showcases, in the next subsections.

We pick up the history of planning in the Netherlands roughly from the start of the Industrial Revolution (i.e., from the 1880s onwards), which started with haphazard residential developments outside the city walls. Planning law was virtually absent or at most very minimalistic and confined to a local scale until this was organized in a more formal and systematic way in the Residential Act of 1901 (*Woningwet*). This Act required the formulation of city extension plans, which led to a period of garden city developments – inspired by Ebenezer Howard's visions on garden cities (Howard *et al.* 1965) – in and around cities such as Rotterdam, Utrecht, Arnhem, Deventer, Hengelo, etc. Besides that, spatial interventions mainly targeted water management, urban development, and the development of waterways and rural areas. This period lasted until the 1940s and was followed by a period of rebuilding the Netherlands following World War II.

In the period between 1945 and 1965, which was characterized by rapid population growth and housing shortages, planning in the Netherlands was further upscaled and professionalized, which is mainly reflected in the installation of the national planning act (*Wet Ruimtelijke Ordening/Besluit ruimtelijke ordening; WRO/Bro*) by 1965. Also, internationally, the Netherlands became well known for the 'Delta works' and large-scale land consolidation projects. In the postwar period, the Netherlands distinguished itself from other countries because of its great social involvement, extensive professionalization, frequent government intervention, and a strong emphasis on national and provincial policy.

So, within the timespan of one century, planning in the Netherlands changed from very minimalistic guidance on the local level to widespread national planning objectives. As we will see, however, this emphasis on either the local level or the national level, on minimal steering or ample guidance, on greenfield development or inner-city redevelopment, etc., is like a pendulum that swings back and forth over time.

1.5.2 'The Dutch created the Netherlands' (1965–1985)

A famous saying is "God created the world, but the Dutch created the Netherlands". This saying is mostly applicable to the period from 1965 until 1985, in which the idea of the 'makeable society' was very prominent in Dutch national policies. In the Dutch welfare state, a prime role was also foreseen for spatial planning. Backed-up with a flourishing economy at that time and the religiously inspired 'pillarization' of society, ambitious visions on the spatial development of the Netherlands were presented – and it was strongly believed that they could be achieved. Of course, this period reflects theoretical notions on blueprint planning (Section 1.4.1) that were dominant in that same time period.

In this period, popular planning concepts in the First and Second National Memorandum on Spatial Planning (*Eerste en Tweede Nota*) of 1958 and 1966 were 'growth centres', the 'Randstad' and 'Green Heart' and 'bundling deconcentration'. This was inspired by the period of rebuilding after World War II, in which high unemployment rates in the rural, agricultural areas in combination with technological developments in the bigger cities led to strong urbanization forces in the western part of the Netherlands. Combined with the economic prosperity and population growth that were mentioned before, there was a strong emphasis on facilitating residential extensions of the cities but, at the same time, preventing uncontrolled and unprecedented urban sprawl.

With the negative images of the 'formless metropolis' of the German Ruhr-area in mind, the national planning policies focused on careful 'managed growth' policies that ensured an equal distribution of people, facilities, employment opportunities, etc., across the entire country. Also, the idea of the polycentric development of the Randstad emerged in this time period. The 'city ring' of the Randstad consisted of Amsterdam, Rotterdam, the Hague, and Utrecht, each city with its own distinctive specialization. These cities could flourish but installing buffer zones in between would prevent the cities from merging with each other and protecting the open, green space in between: the Green Heart. This was supplemented with the 'bundling deconcentration' policy, which coaxed the suburbanization tendencies of the big cities towards specially appointed areas for new town development; the 'growth centres'.

Figure 1.6 Nieuwegein – a typical 1970s satellite town

Illustration: 'growth centre' Nieuwegein

Nieuwegein is a satellite town of the city of Utrecht and was developed in the 1960s and 1970s as part of the 'growth centre' policy, as a response to suburbanization pressure in the Netherlands after World War II (Figure 1.6). It shows how blueprint planning manifests in space. To protect the Dutch 'Green Heart', strategic locations close to the bigger cities were chosen to accommodate the urban populations. Nieuwegein is one of these locations and is famous for its 'cauliflower' neighbourhood development. This is a hierarchical building style aimed at separating the main traffic flows of the city from the inwardly focused residential neighbourhoods. The initial spatial development of

Nieuwegein is a prime example of object-centred planning, where the planners focused on the actual design of the built environment.

In the early 1980s, so towards the end of this planning period, even though 'growth centres' such as Nieuwegein and the 'bundled deconcentration' policy could be considered successful in guiding suburbanization processes, the negative effects of these efforts also became increasingly visible. Economic decline of the bigger cities, in combination with rising unemployment and smaller support for facilities (since the wealthy families mostly moved out of the cities towards the satellite towns) marked the end of the 'makeable society'. Also, commuting between the satellite towns and the employment centres of the big cities led to increasing negative externalities such as congestion and environmental pollution. The pendulum would swing again towards a reorientation on the city, and a reconsideration of the role of the government in planning.

1.5.3 'The Dutch Planner's Paradise' (1985–2010)

As has been already mentioned earlier, the 1990s consisted of a period during which the Netherlands became internationally renowned as the 'Planner's Paradise' because of the large-scale city extensions in the wake of the 'Vinex' policy that were backed by successful public–private partnerships (PPP) between the government and private developers. This period is roughly situated between two economic recessions: starting with the recession of the early 1980s and ending with the global economic collapse of 2010. Responding to the economic crisis of the early 1980s, the position of the government in planning changed drastically from 'director' to 'organizer' and 'facilitator'. It was attempted to guide spatial developments in the Netherlands through cooperation with market parties, preferably on a project basis in PPP structures. This changing role of the government in planning is in line with the 'communicative turn' in planning theory (Section 1.4.2). It marks a shift from a dominant object-orientation towards a dominant process-orientation in planning.

The Third Memorandum on Spatial Planning (*Derde Nota*), which was developed in the 1970s and lasted until the mid-1980s, responded to the negative externalities of the growth centre policy as mentioned before, by investing in urban renewal and introducing the 'compact city' planning concept. The city centres were gradually being renovated and living in the city was made more attractive again in order to slow down suburbanization. The increased urban attention was mainly expressed through socially oriented urban renewal. This meant a thorough renovation of city centres and outdated neighbourhoods in Dutch cities. Key points are densification (the number of buildings per hectare), the restoration of the residential function in the centre (to prevent a dark and lifeless area outside office hours), redevelopment by assigning new functions to existing buildings and redevelopment through demolition and new construction. At the same time, more attention was paid to improving both the old centre and the outskirts of the city through better public transport and the construction of bicycle routes. This halted the trend that had persisted for decades to focus mainly on expanding the urban area. The planning concept of the 'compact city' was thus given substance through better utilization of and more quality in the existing city and to claim as little new space outside the city as possible.

The process of 'reinventing the city' was further stimulated through the Fourth Memorandum on Spatial Planning (*Vierde Nota; 'Vino'*) of 1988 and the Fourth Memorandum – Extra (*Vierde Nota Ruimtelijke Ordening Extra; 'Vinex'*) of 1993. These memoranda consolidated previous planning concepts such as economic competitiveness of the Randstad, preserving the Green Heart and guiding the suburbanization tendencies. Additional emphasis was put on the economic functions of the 'urban nodes', on mainport development (Schiphol Airport and Port of Rotterdam), and on the National Key Projects (*Nationale Sleutelprojecten*; mainly railway station redevelopment projects in the large and middle-sized cities, but also 'flagship projects' such as Kop van Zuid in Rotterdam). A notable difference from the previous policies was the gradually diminishing role of the central government and the growing importance of incorporating market parties on a project basis in PPP constructions. This was particularly reflected in the 'Vinex-locations' – specified areas for residential greenfield development in proximity to the bigger cities. The emphasis shifted from social housing to more market-oriented planning (i.e., 'building for the market'). In this period, many city extensions were realized through PPPs with project developers.

Illustration: 'Vinex-location' Leidsche Rijn

Leidsche Rijn is a suburban city district of Utrecht that resulted from large-scale greenfield development in the 1990s, as part of the 'Vinex' policy' (Figure 1.7). The aim of this policy was to control the urban expansion by selecting greenfield locations close to urban centres that could be used for residential development. These locations were supposed to be both highly accessible by cars, close to motorway

Figure 1.7 Vinex location Leidsche Rijn, Utrecht

exits, and highly accessible by public transport, to have efficient public transport connections to the connected urban centres. This was partly inspired by the idea of transit-oriented development. An important part of the Vinex policy was the shift from government-led planning towards different forms of public–private partnerships. These are essential characteristics of a process-oriented planning approach. Leidsche Rijn is the biggest Vinex location of the Netherlands.

Despite the success and material visibility of the Vinex locations in the Netherlands, the start of the new millennium also marked the start of another **reorientation on planning and the role of the government in the Netherlands.** After a period of market-driven planning and PPPs, the government (mainly the national level and the provinces) was trying to become more prominent again through the Fifth Memorandum on Spatial Planning (*Vijfde Nota*) that was written in 2001. This memorandum, **however**, **never was** formally established by the Dutch parliament, so it had no legal status. The Fifth Memorandum was followed up by the National Memorandum on Spatial Planning (*Nota Ruimte*) in 2004. In this memorandum, in line with the process-domination of this entire planning period, the focus was mainly on governance and the 'how' of national spatial planning. Together with the implementation of this final memorandum, the original planning act of 1965 was also thoroughly revised and updated in 2008 (*Wet op de Ruimtelijke Ordening*). However, as planning always mirrors **societal developments**, yet another phase of planning in the Netherlands was about to commence in response to the spatial implications of the global economic collapse of 2008.

1.5.4 'Paradise Lost?'—New challenges, and a new Act? (2010-present)

A few years after the global economic collapse in 2008, many spatial developments in the Netherlands were also put on hold. It took another couple of years and some governmental incentives such as the Crisis and Recovery Act (*Crisis- en Herstelwet*) before project development and the real estate market were functioning properly again. Dutch land policy also adapted to the post-crisis situation, from the very opportunistic pre-crisis active land policy, in which the government also acted as a private party on the land market, to more facilitating and 'situational' land policies in the years after the crisis, in which financial risks were more carefully weighed against specific other (social) goals of the government. The changes in Dutch land policy are extensively documented elsewhere (e.g., Van Oosten *et al.* 2018), but this change serves as a useful illustration of a shift towards context-orientation that we also noticed in the planning theoretical debate (Section 1.4.3).

This context-orientation not only meant that spatial interventions by the government were becoming more locationally specific. For instance, in this period, the importance of the formal planning system was gradually diminishing, as can be clearly seen in the very minimal role of the national government in the Structural Vision for Infrastructure and Spatial Planning (*Structuurvisie Infrastructuur en Ruimte*) of 2012. In this, it was explicitly stated that urban policies are no longer a national affair, but rather are left to the provinces and municipalities. However, context-orientation also meant that spatial developments were increasingly approached acknowledging the complex societal context in which these challenges were situated, including concerns related to, among other factors, globalization, climate change, economic, and demographic developments.

Finally, context-orientation was also visible in the recent discussions on the Environment and Spatial Planning Act (*Omgevingswet*), which would mark the latest stage of spatial planning in the Netherlands and require a substantial change in the legal and institutional context of planning in the years to come. After a systematic withdrawal of the national administration from the domain of spatial planning since the early crisis years (2008–2010) until now, the installation of the Environment and Spatial Planning Act would mean that the national government would (again) formulate and invest in national spatial policies.

Illustration: urban densification in the Merwedekanaalzone

Utrecht's Merwedekanaalzone reflects this latest phase of land-use planning in the Netherlands, characterized by urban densification and brownfield redevelopment (Figure 1.8). The Merwedekanaalzone is a former brownfield area within the urban fabric of the city of Utrecht that is currently in the process of transformation to a residential area. The aim is to accommodate the increasing housing demand in the city of Utrecht by developing residential locations that are very close to the city centre. High-density land-use is foreseen, as well as low parking norms and an integrated Mobility-as-a-Service concept, with shared mobility services (car-sharing, etc.). The project is largely influenced by the wider societal context such as climate change adaptation and mitigation, energy transition, and the mobility transition.

At the time of writing this book, the development of the Merwedekanaalzone is ongoing. But besides the urban densification goals in this area, the development pressure on the greenfield location of Rijnenburg close to Utrecht is also considerable. It is not unrealistic to think that next to the redevelopment of deteriorated industrial areas such as the Merwedekanaalzone, extensive greenfield development will also become commonplace again in order to keep up with the high demand for housing. In Utrecht, for instance, 10,000 new dwellings are expected to be delivered before 2030. And all of this is taking place in a societal and regulatory context that requires 'greening' of cities, sharper environmental goals, and EU directives on noise, air pollution, etc. It remains to be seen whether Dutch spatial planning will become the victim of its own success.

A final remark on the development of spatial planning in the Netherlands, and the links with planning theory as reflected in the showcases,

Figure 1.8 Utrecht's Merwedekanaalzone

concerns the notion of complementarity. The residential areas of Nieuwegein, Leidsche Rijn, the Merwedekanaalzone, and potentially Rijnenburg in the future are not replacing each other as prime residential locations of the Utrecht city region. Rather, even though they are almost ideal-typical representations of certain crystalized schools of thought in time, they supplement each other and together make up the entire urban landscape of Utrecht. In a similar vein, planning concepts from the national memoranda remain relevant unless they are refuted in future memoranda. For instance, the 'compact city' of the Third Memorandum remains relevant up till today, and the mainports of the 'Vinex' period were already clearly supported in the 'Vino' period. It will become increasingly visible in the years to come how the

Environment and Spatial Planning Act and the National Environmental Vision (*Nationale Omgevingsvisie*; NOVI) will be complementary to this rich history of planning thought, and how this will materialize in future spatial interventions in the Netherlands.

1.6 Conclusion: Entangled theory and practice

The first chapter of this book has introduced the planning triangle as a framework and an analytical tool that provides a structure for understanding planning as a discipline (Spit and Bertolini 1998). The three core elements of this analytical approach are object, process, and context. They represent, respectively: 1) the content of the planning problem, 2) the procedural approach that should lead to a plan that solves the planning problem, and 3) the contextual circumstances in which this discussion takes place.

This chapter has also shown how the dimensions of the planning triangle link with planning theory. In recent debates on planning theory, this threefold perspective of context, object and process has been increasingly recognized: "A narrow definition of planning theory results in theoretical weakness arising from the isolation of process from context and outcome" (Fainstein 2005, p. 121). In other words, planning needs to take these three dimensions explicitly into account (Figure 1.9). The object–process–context interrelation is used here as an analytical framework for positioning theoretical views (Hartmann and Geertman 2016).

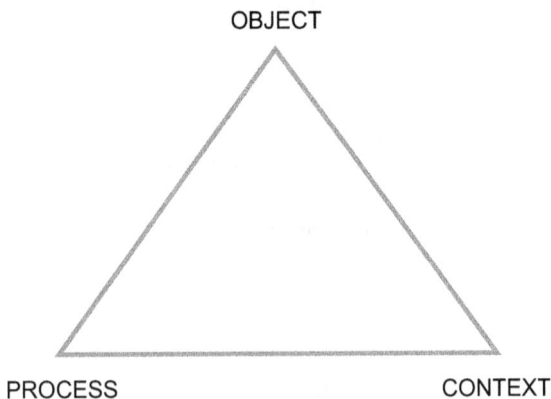

Figure 1.9 The planning triangle

Although the planning triangle should not be projected on every planning issue in a very absolutist way, at least analytically, all variables of a planning issue can hypothetically be grouped at some point within the triangle. All variables related to the "what" fall under the category of object variables, such as location, type, quantity, variation, and quality. Process variables ("how and who") relate to types of actors, interests, resources, and lead time. Finally, the context variables stem from the institutional setting (planning system), social and cultural trends, and economic developments. The planning triangle is not striving to be a comprehensive method to deconstruct all planning issues into mutually exclusive sets of clearly defined variables. It can rather be regarded as **an analytical tool** that is useful for better understanding the complexity of spatial problems and as a conceptual tool for better structuring spatial planning interventions.

We can thus conclude from this chapter that spatial planning can be seen as a public activity on the comprehensive future of space. It provides an idea of how a certain territory shall develop in the future. To better understand, explain, and potentially structure and intervene in spatial planning practice, the planning triangle can be helpful as an analytical tool to discern what is happening in integrated, complex planning challenges (i.e., 'wicked problems'). The next three chapters therefore each investigate one element of this planning triangle.

2 The object of planning
Land-use

In this chapter, the **object of planning** is at the centre of attention. First, the key characteristics of the object of planning are presented. Subsequently, land-use planning is discussed in relation to the object, which is then related to different spatial scales. Based on this, a section is dedicated to exploring the relevance of the planning object with some examples from Dutch planning practice, particularly related to strategic planning of large-scale infrastructures, as such projects provide prime examples of the complexity of the planning object and its relations with and implications for the process and context of planning.

2.1 The object of planning: five key characteristics

The object of planning at large describes **what is planned** (such as the housing stock, business parks, office locations, the motorway network, etc.). Planning affects the allocation and distribution of scarce spatial resources, namely land (Davy 2005; Needham 2006). The object of planning can be conceived as the spatial resources that planning is dealing with, such as the built environment and landscapes – houses, offices, stores, but also nature, agriculture, roads, etc.; beyond that, though, it also encompasses land, related land values and rights to the land, which affect the way land is used. Often this land must be prepared and serviced before its functions can be developed (Buitelaar and Witte 2011). These functions and real estates are connected through traditional (i.e., roads) and critical (i.e., energy, sewage, etc.) infrastructure systems and networks. The infrastructure system is hence also part of the object of planning (Witte 2014). So, there are many different elements of planning objects (real estate, land, infrastructures, etc.).

Spatial planning is – in most countries – growth-oriented (Davy 2006; Needham 2014; Hartmann and Gerber 2018; Stöglehner 2020).

DOI: 10.4324/9781003230489-2

This means that one of the core tasks of planning is the provision of building land for different land-uses and spatial interests. Because of the growth orientation of planning, the object of planning can be better understood by exploring **land economics and land markets** (Needham 2006), sometimes referred to in literature as 'economics of property development' (e.g., Guy and Henneberry 2002). In terms of land economics, this differentiation of the object of planning has led to many scattered so-called 'sub-markets' with vague boundaries that are sometimes overlapping and sometimes mutually exclusive, for instance, 'the real estate market of the Amsterdam South Axis' or 'the housing sector in the Utrecht region'. This can also result in vague and untransparent definitions of what constitutes spatial planning and land-use.

We identify **five key characteristics** of the object of planning, including the following: 1) the physical connection of an object to a location, 2) the inert nature of the object, 3) the heterogeneity of the object, 4) the functional possibilities of the object, and 5) the price of the object. In the following sections, we briefly outline each of the five key characteristics.

2.1.1 *The physical connection of an object to a location (1)*

One of the most obvious characteristics of the object is the physical connection of the object to one geographical **location**. For land this is of course even more fixed than for buildings, but in general the 'place attachment' of the object can be regarded as a generally accepted characteristic of the object. This characteristic has two important implications.

First, from the supply side, this implies that, at some locations, the land assets will be claimed for a prolonged period, making it unavailable for alternative uses. In economic theory, such a characteristic of scarcity is related to the concept of rivalrousness that distinguishes public or club goods from common and private goods (Hess and Ostrom 2007). At the same time, we see that in land-use planning this feature of immovability is also utilized in strategic ways (Gerber *et al.* 2017). The physical connection of an object to a location is also closely related to the inert nature of the object (i.e., the second characteristic). This implies that the effective supply of real estate – or other land-uses – is only a very limited part of the total hypothetical supply. In literature, this is referred to as the 'stock market' nature of the real estate market (e.g., Glaeser *et al.* 2008). Because of the place attachment of land-uses, the **supply of land-uses is rather inelastic,** meaning that even if demand would sharply increase, the supply will only increase to a very limited degree, leading to quickly increasing prices.

Second, from the demand side, the **place attachment of land-uses also has consequences.** In contrast to other transferable goods, in this case the customer goes to the product, instead of the product coming to the customer. Looking at land markets, this leads to spatial segmentation that is crystalized in regional sub-markets. These sub-markets are not fixed, meaning that the construction of infrastructure can lead to serious fluctuations in housing demand due to improved accessibility. For instance, in the Netherlands, a future construction of the long-debated 'Zuiderzeelijn' or 'Lelylijn' – a high-speed passenger railway line that would connect the Amsterdam Metropolitan Area to the peripheral, northern parts of the country – could have significant effects on the balance between housing supply and demand at both ends of this railway line, and consequently also influence future real estate prices.

2.1.2 The inert nature of the object (2)

Ellickson (1993) emphasizes that private ownership of land "promotes individual liberty, political stability, and economic prosperity" (p. 1317). Changing land that once has been assigned to a certain land-use can be difficult and costly. In other words, land and its associated property rights are very robust institutions. The buildings themselves on average last some 50 to a hundred years. Note that this is embedded in some language – the German term for real estate is '*Immobilie*'; it entails the notion of immovability. Also, economically, mortgages and real estate financing are long-term and tardy in response. Combined with the place attachment of land-use, the 'stock market' nature of the land market as referred to before is inert as well. This is very important for setting the prices on the market and for the return for investors on the real estate market. Altogether, this leads to a **robust, irreversible, immovable, and inert nature** of land, being the primary object of planning (Van Straalen *et al.* 2018).

2.1.3 The heterogeneity of the object (3)

In principle, land can never be fully identical to the other locations, for the very simple reason that every location is different from another. Different land-uses can either look alike, or be completely different from one another, leading to a different price setting for every piece of land-use. Comparing land prices is therefore a complicated task, and nation-wide average sales figures do not reveal much about the specific circumstances of one single land-use object. In combination with the inert nature of the object, this means that – over time – common standards of what is regarded as a 'spacious' house can even change substantially. This reinforces the **heterogeneity and locational context-specificity** of the object, as the examples of the spatial layouts of Nieuwegein, Leidsche Rijn, and the Merwedekanaalzone in the previous chapter have already illustrated.

2.1.4 The functional possibilities of the object (4)

Following the heterogeneity of the object, the land market can be further sub-divided into different functions, such as residential use, commercial use, retail use, etc. This translates into different functional sub-markets, such as the residential market, office market, etc. The boundaries of these sub-markets are usually clearly distinguishable and are therefore not easily interchangeable. Substantial modifications to real estate are hard to implement, as can be seen in the societal discussion that is already going on for years on transforming vacant office buildings into residential units. Such transformations are further complicated by the fact that many **functional uses are spatially bounded.** For instance, many office buildings are in industrial areas or along motorways, making a transformation into residential units rather unlikely (e.g., because of restrictive zoning regulations).

2.1.5 The price of the object (5)

The **price of the object,** and in particular the price setting, is one of the most remarkable characteristics of the **land and real estate markets** (Buitelaar and Witte 2011). In general, the price for real estate is rather high, amongst many other reasons mostly influenced by scarcity. Building costs and the possibility to spread the financing over a longer period are also important explanations for the high prices. Because of this last reason, the real estate market is also an important 'competitor' on the capital assets market. This means that the return on investment of real estate relative to other capital assets, and the spreading of risk, become major drivers for decisions to invest in real estate. The global economic collapse of 2008 and, more recently, the economic shockwaves due to the worldwide COVID-19 pandemic have proven that the factor of 'trust' is easily underestimated in the capital asset market and therefore also in the land market.

Two specific points are worth noting here. First, it should be noted that there is an analytical **difference between price and value.** The price is the actual transaction price of a piece of land or real estate. The value or the valuation of land or real estate is a much more normative endeavour (Dey Biswas 2020), influenced by many factors (e.g., Buitelaar and Witte 2011, for a further elaboration on the residual valuation method that is often used in Dutch land-use planning). Furthermore, the government is also playing a role in the price setting and development of prices on the real estate markets, for instance through policy instruments such as subsidizing, taxes, or active land policy (i.e., land acquisition and land distribution; Gerber *et al.* 2018).

Taken together, these **five key characteristics of the object of planning** result in the unique and place-bound nature of the object that can literally vary from one block of houses to the next. This means that the land market is also very different relative to other types of markets (e.g., the financial market). This unique character of the object of planning and the related particularities of land markets have implications for how spatial planning and land-use planning are organized. This is further explored in the next sections.

2.2 Spatial planning and land-use planning

In the literature, the **relation between spatial planning and land-use planning** is not unambiguous: "Present day spatial planning began with something called urban planning, or land-use planning, or town-and-country planning" (Hartmann and Needham 2012, p. 1). In the international literature, there is semantic confusion between spatial planning on one side and land-use planning or zoning, on the other side.

Land-use planning refers to binding regulations on the way land may be used. In some countries – in particular in North America – land-use planning is commonly referred to as zoning (Sclar *et al.* 2020). The central instrument of land-use planning is the binding land-use plan, which comes with different names in different countries – such as zoning plan (United States), development plan (United Kingdom), *Bebauungsplan* (Germany), *bestemmingsplan*, or *omgevingsplan* (the Netherlands). Despite some differences in form and exact legal status, these documents provide a legally binding nature in most EU countries for landowners to know what they may or may not do with their properties (Albrechts 2004). Land-use plans also regulate the rights of others (such as access to the land or other obligations) (Hartmann and Needham 2012). This legal certainty requires predictability and reliability. Land-use planning is therefore often characterized using numerical standards, such as the residential building density per square kilometre or the floor space index. These are often formulated as simplified and schematized rules on certain qualitative and quantitative aspects of organizing our society via land-use planning.

In contrast to land-use planning, **spatial planning** is mostly conceived as a more strategic and ambitious type of planning, and oftentimes also more integral. This is referred to as comprehensive, integrated, or strategic spatial planning (e.g., Hersperger *et al.* 2019). Spatial planning is hence more concerned with the strategic planning of entire cities or even metropolitan regions. As the title of this book suggests, the focus here is more strictly on spatial planning and the more strategic orientation towards the planning of cities and regions. Therefore, this book only pays modest attention to land-use planning in the sense of (the content of) municipal zoning plans and related legal procedures. For further reading on this, we refer to Gerber *et al.* (2018), Needham *et al.* (2018), and Needham (2014). As will be further explored in the next chapter, we see (strategic) spatial planning as very instrumental in the more informal planning phases prior to the formalization of a legally binding land-use or zoning plan. Considering the increasing uncertainty of the societal context of planning (Chapter 4), the strategic orientation of spatial planning is deemed as crucial in our present-day society to arrive at ambitious spatial plans with enough political and societal support.

2.2.1 Different perspectives on the development of land-use

In the Netherlands, the use of either of both approaches (spatial planning or land-use planning) shows **variability over time**, in other words, in some periods concrete land-use planning is more dominant, whereas in other periods strategic spatial planning is more dominant. This is influenced by the dominant perspective on how land-use planning should be conducted.

Land-use planning is concerned with two main questions regarding the development and allocation of land-uses: 1) what are the spatial claims (i.e., what functions is the land to fulfil? How much space do they take?) and 2) what are the potential locations (i.e., where can the functions be realized?). In literature and practice, **different perspectives on land-use planning co-exist** that differ in their emphasis on either the spatial claims or on the potential locations. For instance, Buitelaar (2012) distinguishes development-led plans, conservation plans, and steering plans. There are two aspects that are relevant to discuss here: the first is a managed growth perspective that can be reflected in either development-led plans or in steering plans; the second is a conservation planning perspective (with the associated conservation plans).

Managed growth/development-led planning (1)

The central premise of the managed growth approach is that new developments should be given the **opportunity to be developed**, making use of existing space and infrastructure that is already available at a certain location. At the same time, certain spaces or corridors need to be left open to anticipate future developments in this area. Buitelaar (2012) denotes such plans as development-led plans, if the plan is linked with concrete implementation (typical in Dutch active land policy), and steering plans, if the future realization is still open and the plan provides mere strategic directions. This implies that, while making use of existing space and infrastructure, new structures also need to be developed simultaneously to accommodate this potential future growth. In practice, however, these two aspects of land-use planning (i.e., development-led planning and strategic orientations on future spatial developments) do not run parallel, and oftentimes infrastructures only follow once other land-uses are already developed. The development of the large-scale greenfield residential area of Leidsche Rijn near Utrecht is a prime example of this. This is an important challenge to consider from a managed growth perspective on land-use planning.

Planning for conservation (2)

This contrasting perspective on land-use planning is primarily concerned with **conservation of the existing land-uses**. Also, for this perspective, two types of planning can be further distinguished:

1. *Contraction*: this is used to stop deterioration of neighbourhoods, by means of regulations and active interventions in the market. For instance: selling rental housing to the tenants, to improve the balance between the rental housing stock and the privately owned properties in a certain neighbourhood. As active intervention, redeveloping the public spaces can be considered.
2. *Conservation*: protecting the – oftentimes historical – qualities. For instance, protecting the townscape by means of regulations, putting historical buildings on a heritage conservation list, etc.

These models are ideal-typical approaches to addressing and categorizing land-use planning. Although such standardized approaches and their related numerical standards (e.g., on densities, proximity of functions, or rather separation thereof) are still often used as guidelines or generic values to determine the size and scope of building programs (e.g., plot sizes per building type, relative proportions of functions, etc.), such approaches often fail to properly consider the complexity of land-use. The **complexity of land-use** complicates efficient and reproducible land-use planning practices, as will be illustrated in the next section.

2.2.2 The complexity of land-use

Spatial planning decides on how land and buildings should be used (Needham *et al.* 2018). The complexity of such decisions results from different and competing spatial quantitative and qualitative demands by different stakeholders under circumstances of scarcity. Stakeholders can be existing or future users (consider residents of an area and the construction of an adjacent highway), but they can also represent spatial interests, such as cultural heritage or nature. The notion of scarcity is thereby crucial. "Scarcity is usually thought to be found in situations where limited resources are confronted with demands (or needs) that outreach the available supply" (Hartmann and Gerber 2018). Scarcity of land is not a (mere) natural characteristic of space, but it is rather socially constructed as a result of political processes. For example, the protection of a natural area creates scarcity, while the designation of additional building land for a certain land-use alleviates scarcity for a specific sector. **Without scarcity of land, spatial planning becomes obsolete.**

The professional and academic literature attempts to capture land-use, its change, and its characteristics through **quantitative or semi-quantitative methods.** Urban economics tries to understand land-uses based on land rent models or appraisal of land-uses, real estate investors try to assess opportunities with cost-benefit analyses, and sectoral planning explores land-use alternatives with multi-criteria analysis (Needham *et al.* 2018). Such approaches, however, cannot fully capture the complex reality of land-use resulting from scarcity of land (Davy 2012; Dey Biswas 2020).

How does planning then deal with this complexity? While early approaches to spatial planning applied the quantitative and semi-quantitative methods to develop a rational-comprehensive plan, contemporary spatial planning approaches often pursue a more incrementalistic approach that is more sensitive to the particularities of a certain spatial intervention and its potentially suitable locations. Important considerations are, for instance, as follows:

- Is there a need to create or maintain a certain space within a potential location, for instance for nature conservation or climate change protection (e.g., flooding)?
- Do any existing structures within the landscape need to be maintained (for instance existing buildings, infrastructures, green spaces)?
- How much space needs to be reserved for necessary spatial functions that come along with, for example, residential development? These could be streets, main roads, schools, local shops, medical services, green spaces, etc.

The questions of 'what', 'how much', and 'where' guide the planning and design of urban land-use, and its complexity. When such questions are answered, the planning process usually starts with finding the 'right' locations based on an inventory of locational requirements and a general idea of the spatial claims. For potentially interesting locations, a first spatial design will then be sketched. This in turn leads to a critical examination of the spatial claims considering the specific possibilities or hindrances of this location. Ultimately, the core elements of the building programme are translated into a spatial design or sketch of the location. Which functions will be realized and where? How are they positioned relative to each other and relative to the surroundings (i.e., what are the 'relational patterns' between functions)? How much space do they occupy?

The core elements of the building programme are in the end determined by **(political) preferences and choices** of the socio-spatial distribution of functions, for instance regarding the type and quantity of residential units. These choices are formalized in the 'real' urban design plan. Such decisions about the building programme are often translated into the land balance. The land balance is a schematic overview of the building programme and related costs and revenues of land development that provides the basis for a financial calculation of the building programme (Buitelaar and Witte 2011). This latter calculation is often formalized into municipal land servicing accounts.

2.3 Land-use planning at different spatial scales

In many countries, spatial planning is embedded in **institutions at different tiers of government**. In some countries – for example, for nation states within the European Union – additional supranational spatial claims can play a role too, though the European Union does not have a formal competency on spatial planning (Hartmann and Hengstermann 2014). Sometimes, the tiers of government are in competition with each other (e.g., in France), sometimes they are organized in a nested system of subsidiarity (such as in Germany; Reimer *et al.* 2014). Some systems have both competing and nested elements embedded in their planning systems, such as in the Netherlands.

At the **national level** (or state level in federally organized countries), spatial planning often remains in the form of guidelines for locations and general principles for land-use. Sometimes specific locations are mentioned, but oftentimes this still incorporates considerable degrees of freedom for lower levels of government (according to the principle of subsidiarity, see Chapter 4). At the **regional level** (in the Netherlands: the provinces), national planning principles are translated into strategic provincial visions. Also, here, some specific 'explorative locations' can be indicated with some degrees of freedom for the municipalities to determine the final locations. The municipal level is the most important one, as the legally binding land-use plans are prepared at this level (although in the Netherlands and some other countries as well, other tiers of government can also determine land-use plans or special plan procedures that are binding for landowners).

It is at the **local scale** where the questions on the 'what', 'where', and 'how much' of land-use are specified and confrontations between relevant stakeholders take place on supply and demand of land-use. However, the local scale is not isolated from influence by and **dynamic interactions with other spatial scales**. The scalar issue is an inherent part of studying the object of planning. From the foregoing discussion, it has already become apparent that obvious links must be made with the process and context of planning at different spatial scales. For the sake of clarity, we will limit the discussion to some notions about scale from an object-oriented point of view. This section thus briefly outlines various considerations concerning the planning of land-use at the various relevant scale levels.

2.3.1 National level

At the national level, the **primary goal is to steer the development** of the main physical (infra-) structure. This relates to important decisions regarding the main structure of the motorway network, the freight- and (high-speed) railway networks, and the development possibilities for airport or ports. Sectoral spatial policies at the national level can influence spatial planning quite substantially by claiming space for certain spatial functions, such as water management, energy, or nature conservation. However, the direct influence on specific locations and spatial claims is in practice rather limited.

However, only when **significant financial investments** on the part of the national government are concerned, the national government can have considerable influence on concrete locational decisions or spatial claims too, for example, the Dutch Vinex-policy (Section 1.5), which determined spatial development for specific locations with certain mandatory requirements of the national government (e.g., building density) that developers needed to adhere to. Other examples of such national influence, also outside of the formal domain of spatial planning, include the financing of primary education or financial incentives to stimulate the liveability of rural areas.

2.3.2 Regional level

Regional planning develops spatial visions beyond the local scale, while at the same time specifying national planning concepts, such as the concept of 'bundled deconcentration' from the 1970s, transit-oriented developments, or urban-growth boundaries (e.g., Dieleman and Wegener 2004). More locationally specific concepts are the concept of the Green Heart, describing a vast open space area in the Dutch Randstad (Van der Valk and Faludi 1997), or a regional green belt system in the Ruhr area (Wegener 2012; Macdonald *et al.* 2021). For several special land-use functions with regional relevance, such as solar parks or wind turbines, regional planning authorities sometimes designate specific locations and conditions, with some manoeuvring space for the exact size and scope of the development at these sites. Thereby oftentimes, "the regional tier functions rather with collaboration and consultation then through enforcement" (Janssen-Jansen and Tan 2018, p. 138).

2.3.3 Local level

At the local (municipal) level, land-uses are influenced by **legally binding land-use plans.** These plans grant, confirm, or confine what a landowner may or may not do with his or her land. Traditionally, land-use plans pursue a functional separation of land-uses that conflict each other. In 1926, the US Supreme Court, in its decision of the village of Euclid against Amber Realty Co. clarified that a land-use is not per se good or bad, but it can be simply misplaced. Planning, as the court decision explained, is about avoiding nuisances: "a nuisance may be merely a right thing in the wrong place, – like a pig in the parlour instead of the barnyard" (US Supreme Court decision 1926 on the village of Euclid vs. Ambler Realty Co.). This led to the term Euclidian zoning (Sclar *et al.* 2020). Although this perspective is rather libertarian, in the sense that the aim of planning is to protect property, it explains the rationale of functional separation of land-uses.

In the European context, **functional separation** stems from the more utilitarian perspective of avoiding serious harm to cities by preventing fires, providing healthy living conditions, etc. Today, such notions of functional separation are deeply rooted in planning legislation and beyond (Dembski 2020). The functional separation can either be specific or more open. The degree of specificness or openness of the land-use regulations provides or confines the material flexibility of a plan (Van den Hoek *et al.* 2020), which in the end is relevant in the attempt to clarify to citizens, businesses, etc., to what extent certain land-uses are legally protected or allow for more flexibility. For instance, larger areas of the plan can be designated for residential purposes, business purposes, infrastructures, green areas, etc., with only limited rules and regulations for what is allowed and what not. An example of such a more open land-use plan is the land-use plan for Oosterwold, close to Almere in the Netherlands (Van Straalen *et al.* 2017).

2.3.4 Multi-level dynamics

The previous explanations may suggest that there is a **linear relation throughout the different tiers and scales of spatial planning**. At the higher scale levels, land-use is generally considered in a more abstract sense, as providing guidelines or spatial visions, whereas the municipal level is usually the strongest, where binding land-use decisions are made on specific plots of land. This seems to suggest a 'trickling down' effect of abstract and generic concepts at the national level all the way down into the locally binding land-use plan. However, the reality of spatial planning is less hierarchical. Instead, principles of countervailing and subsidiarity influence and characterize the mutual relationships between national, regional, and local planning. To illustrate, regional and national authorities can intervene directly in local land-use planning and release binding plans. As mentioned, such mechanisms and multi-level dynamics will be further explained in the subsequent chapters on process and context. The next section will show the complexity of mutual relations in the planning system from an object-oriented perspective, using the example of large-scale infra-structure development.

2.4 Land-use and scale: planning large-scale infrastructures

As mentioned in the beginning of this chapter, the object of planning has a very diverse nature, of which **infrastructure development** is one of the functional land-uses. This section by means of illustration high-lights the planning of and investments in large-scale infrastructures as a clear case of the complexity of the object of planning and its relation to the process and context of planning, which will be discussed in more detail in the upcoming chapters.

2.4.1 Investing in large-scale infrastructure development

It is argued that infrastructure development is **one of the major forces supporting the spatial dynamics of contemporary urban regions** (Hanson and Giuliano 2004). Infrastructure development is especially much needed as the physical 'condition' supporting the multitude of socio-economic processes, freight and passenger transport flows, the development of urban cultures, etc., that occur in urban regions (Graham and Marvin 2002). At the same time, it is argued that the location of infrastructure itself exerts an influence on urbanization patterns and economic development (Priemus *et al.* 2001). On the one hand, societal developments encourage new types of economic activi-ties, which in turn affect the demands placed on the existing economic (transport) infrastructure. On the other hand, societal developments and the associated new economic activities provide new opportuni-ties to improve the economic infrastructure itself. This is, for instance, clearly illustrated in the literature on Transit-Oriented Development (TOD) (e.g., Cervero 2004; Bertolini *et al.* 2012).

As an object of planning, **investing in large-scale infrastructure development is much debated** for its complex relation with urban and economic development. It is widely believed that investing in infra-structure generates effects on the (potential) economic development of metropolitan areas. On the one hand, many academics argue that a strong mutual interdependency exists between the development of transport infrastructures and the growth of regional economic systems (e.g., Cervero 2004). On the other hand, others emphasize the lack of empirical proof for net effects on a higher level of scale, as new infrastructure reduces the cost of both import and export of goods and services. Instead, they point at the economic cost of external effects such as noise, congestion, and emissions (Knaap and Oosterhaven 2003). There is no overall conclusion, showing the complexity of the relation.

Also, in the Netherlands, the issue of **economic effects of transport infrastructure investment** gained attention, by emphasizing in spatial policies the phenomenon of urban networks, namely groups of independent cities that work together to improve spatial and economic development (Priemus 2007). This policy focus on strengthening the large metropolitan areas and the relations between them dates back to the 1990s when the concept of the compact city was introduced (Dieleman *et al*. 1999). Also, in recently published plans (e.g., *Topsector Logistiek*), it is reflected that these ideas are still very dominant in the Netherlands. Such spatial and economic policies are consistent with a generally shared belief that economic growth is especially fuelled by economic activities in major urban areas (Fujita and Thisse 2002), and the underlying assumption that investing in the infrastructure is an important condition, necessary to sustain economic growth. In other words, transport infrastructure is dependent on economic development and vice versa (Rietveld and Nijkamp 2000).

This is, however, not the only **important feature of investments in infrastructure**. It is also important for the development of spatial structures and the determination of mobility (Short and Kopp 2005). By their very nature and connectivity, transport networks create comparative advantages and disadvantages for areas and industries regarding the conditions of accessibility, locational qualities, responsiveness to markets, and the flexibilities of scale (Bertolini 1999). In this discussion, the argument is often heard that the economic benefits of infrastructure developments are larger in the central urban areas than elsewhere, for more households and firms can and are likely to use the new facilities. Furthermore, advocates from this view argue that, in the slipstream of these investments, social problems in the cities can be tackled as well. On the other hand stands the classic argument that any investment in areas where there are little or no facilities at all, the (marginal) economic effects are much larger than elsewhere (Hansen 1968).

2.4.2 *The structuring effects of infrastructure: space and time*

It can be concluded that infrastructure as an object of planning potentially has structuring effects for **urban and economic**

developments. There are two issues that specifically stress such structuring effects (Bruijn *et al.* 1996): the problem of location (where will it be located) and the problem of time (which causes uncertainty). In the long run, the improvement of infrastructure can lead to a change in spatial structures (Bruinsma *et al.* 1997). However, it is difficult to determine the lines of causality, as both processes are related. The relations can be of a different nature, as infrastructure development not only improves the attainability of cities and regions but also opens a way out for residents and companies within the same city or region (i.e., backwash effects). Also, the relations are not always as linear as is sometimes suggested.

The spatial structuring **effects of infrastructure development are twofold.** As the attainability of cities and regions improves, flows of traffic will tend to change. New opportunities for economic growth arise, which in turn will affect traffic. This development has consequences for transportation time, attainability of the city or region and its reliability. A second structuring effect is the possible (re-)adjustment of economic activities in the same city or region. The regional real estate market in general benefits from infrastructural improvements. This accounts as well for housing markets as for more commercial types of real estate.

However, the question **which spatial, economic, or social development is a direct result from infrastructure development** can hardly be answered. First, as mentioned, causality is hard to determine. Next, there is the problem of spatial scales. Infrastructure development and improvement often takes place at more than one spatial level. The simple distinction between (inter-)national-, regional-, and local levels no longer suffices here, because this distinction cannot cope with the complexity of intermodality, as different modes of transport tend to concentrate their activities on different spatial levels. Third, time is essential. The real effect of infrastructure development – in a positive sense – gradually materializes in time. From a short-term perspective, this implies that the costs of development are highly visible – including all inconveniences and NIMBY behaviour in the development stage – versus the suggested benefits and low costs in a long-term perspective. Finally, there is the problem of spatial substitution, which focuses on the question whether (from a public perspective) the development of new infrastructure generates new economic activities or merely causes the relocation of existing ones within the region. This discussion thus highlights the complexity of infrastructure as an object of planning and can be further illustrated by zooming in on a particular Dutch case study in the next sub-section.

2.4.3 *Dutch example: the Betuweroute and the German hinterland*

As an illustration of the complexity of infrastructure as an object of planning, we zoom in to the Dutch case study of the **Betuweroute** and its troublesome connections to the German hinterland. This illustration is based on a case study conducted by one of the authors of this book (Witte 2014, pp. 147–148) but remains relevant. It highlights the discussion with respect to the creation of a third railway track in Germany between Emmerich and Oberhausen to better connect the dedicated Dutch freight transport railway line Betuweroute to the German hinterland. This railway line holds strategic importance as a freight corridor connecting the port of Rotterdam to the Ruhr region in Germany. Whereas the Dutch government has speeded up the procedure for implementation of this project, the German procedure is running parallel but without strict deadlines for implementation, for national political reasons. This is likely to hamper the implementation of fluent cross-border freight transport in the short term.

The German rail operator Deutsche Bahn has therefore developed a project to upgrade the railway line to three tracks and eliminate most of the level crossings. According to German law, the new development should provide the necessary compensations to communities, including noise reduction measures (i.e., noise walls). However, due to the topographical structure of the area and the type of settlements, these walls need to be high (often between two and six metres). This has encountered the opposition of communities that see the proposed solution as a further disturbance to their living conditions rather than their betterment.

At first sight, **this seems to be merely an infrastructure problem**; the German part of the network following the Betuweroute appears to be lacking in capacity, so an additional railway track is needed at one specific section of the network. However, closer examination also reveals problems with respect to transnational governance: political resistance to the project, and differences in institutional structures and procedures that hamper efficient cross-border cooperation. Moreover, the German section of the line presents several additional problems that need to be solved: some 50 level crossings along the line, the insufficient capacity of the stations (e.g., Oberhausen) or sub-optimal employment of the nodes, and disturbances to the surrounding settlements (e.g., noise, dangerous materials, fragmentation of communities).

First, it should be noted that **many aspects are interrelated in this case**. What at first sight seems to be a mere infrastructure problem also appears to have clear spatial, environmental, political, and institutional dimensions. In addition, the issues occur on multiple levels of scale. On a local level, the project of the Deutsche Bahn is facing heavy resistance because of the visual impact of the noise walls. On the other hand, from a transnational perspective, this area is of crucial importance to achieve efficient freight transport from the Betuweroute to the German hinterland. Thus, different issues interfere at different spatial scales. This calls for a set of strategic measures.

A second point of concern is the **modal competition** this area is facing. On the one hand, the creation of a third track to solve the problems should be measured against the alternative costs of expanding the German motorway network. The ongoing policy attitude towards achieving modal shift from transport by road to rail and inland navigation is helpful and strategic in this respect, to strengthen the insufficient and difficult links between the railway and the inland ports in this region. On the other hand, inland navigation itself via the river Rhine can also be seen as a competitor to rail transport for this area. Moreover, this line is in competition with other transportation routes that show high rates of transported tons/km and with other projects that also vie for German federal funding. In this way, economic potential can also be included as a factor of importance, to add to the complexity of the area.

Two strategic questions can be posed regarding this region. First, should the project concentrate only on the creation of a third track and the realization of noise protection on a local scale to solve the bottlenecks, or are there more strategic interventions to be implemented in this region? Second, is noise protection the only way to tackle the existing environmental bottlenecks, or can upgrades to the railway station areas and their surroundings lead to synergies on a regional scale that can be seen as a form of compensation?

In the first question, the **negative external effects**, which tend to aggregate on a low spatial scale (i.e., noise nuisance, safety and visual quality of the localities involved), are measured against possible positive spill-over effects, which tend to aggregate on a higher spatial scale (e.g., corridor development and related regional economic growth). The second question makes use of a **growth management perspective:** in this case, compensating noise nuisance with the creation of synergies at railway station areas. In this way, the attempt is made to solve transport, spatial, and environmental issues on a local scale by seeking economic potential on a regional to transnational scale. The research problem thus evolves from a short-term technical transportation issue to a problem of long-term economic development and possible spatial planning interventions.

In summary, the **strategic questions that were posed** can contribute to the creation of an alternative regional and integrated spatial planning perspective on the future development of this region. With such a strong focus on the local noise problem and related land-use solutions, the regional development perspective had been lost. This is not to say that technical solutions to technical bottlenecks are therefore irrelevant, but by adopting this integrated spatial planning perspective, new opportunities and development alternatives have come to the fore. The case study also clearly shows the problems of space and time related to infrastructure development and the relation of the object of planning with the associated planning process and planning context.

2.5 Discussion: scale and scarcity in Dutch land-use planning

The first chapter introduced **spatial planning as the 'mirror of society'**. Throughout this chapter, the characteristics of the object of planning and land-use planning have been discussed from this perspective. In doing so, we have witnessed a growing complexity of land-use because of increasingly competing interests of actors over a limited amount of (mainly urban) space. A point of discussion that remains is the issue of scarcity. This is also partly a normative discussion. For many years, every now and then the phrase 'the Netherlands is full' has recurred in societal and political debates. However, when actual land-use is considered, over half of the available land in the Netherlands is still occupied by agricultural uses, whereas only one-fifth of the total area is used for urbanization, including infrastructures. Even though a shift in the availability and distribution of buildable land for urbanization could theoretically be realized (i.e., designating agricultural sites for urban purposes outside of the Randstad area, and accepting the increased mobility flows that would follow), it is doubtful whether that will occur. This is because the compact city concept (Dieleman and Wegener 2004) has been prominent in Dutch land-use policies over the past 30 years. This bundling of urban functions and facilities, which is currently promoted as 'inner-city densification', has led to scarcity of buildable urban land and increased prices for land and real estate development.

The issue of **scarcity is therefore always a matter of perception**. When scarcity is viewed from an international perspective, in which the Randstad area or the Netherlands is viewed in relative comparison to, for example, Paris, London, or Istanbul, or in comparison to many Asian cities, then the Netherlands can be seen as a scarcely populated urban area. From this international perspective, high-rise development is virtually absent in the Netherlands, and densities are rather low. What remains from that perspective is an attractive (semi-)urban landscape with surrounding green areas that are quickly and easily accessible to everyone (also the peripheral nature reserves). On the other hand, were one to view the Netherlands as a primarily agricultural country (and the land-use distribution would qualify as such), then it could also be viewed as a densely populated rural area, in which the urbanization pressure is high. The conclusion that there is only limited space for large-scale agricultural companies would then be justified.

It is very important to be aware of the potential spatial policy implications of such **normative viewpoints on the urbanity** of the Netherlands. Why would multi-functional land-use or subterranean building be considered viable options when this would not come from a perspective of scarcity of buildable land? It is interesting to observe how such notions on scarcity develop over time, also in relation to periods of economic recession. All in all, it is important to be sensitive to the deeper layer of normative assumptions in analyzing and assessing the current state of Dutch land-use planning.

2.6 Conclusion: increasing normativity

The object of planning is of interest to geographers and spatial planners alike. However, what distinguishes spatial planners is that they do not only want to analyze or understand the object, but they also continually want to intervene in practice and change the object of planning in the light of ongoing societal developments. The right functions need to be developed at the right locations, and this is a continuous and iterative process. This chapter has provided some guidelines as to how to do this. For example, residential development is of interest for spatial planners, larger residential areas such as the Dutch Vinex locations. Important questions that also need to be answered are how to accommodate infrastructures, green spaces, schools, shops, facilities, etc. Proximity and separation are important factors to consider in (residential) land-use planning. For instance, related to residential development: proximity of a primary school vs. separation of industrial pollution. Related to this, the concept of (residential) density is also important, often crystalized in standardized units (e.g., building density per square hectare), as well as the spatial scale at which 'density' is considered. For instance, regional differences might be considerable.

All of this is leading to increasing normativity in the object of planning. What follows from this is that the physical location of the object is of prime importance for any kind of land development and should be the first consideration of any spatial development process. It is to the process that our attention will turn in the upcoming chapter.

3   The process of planning
Policy and governance

After discussing the object of planning in the previous chapter, this chapter explores the process of planning. This means that the 'How?' question is central to this chapter. Planning processes are not independent of the location-specific problem itself (the object) and the (institutional) conditions in which the planning process should take place (the context). Though political and administrative science feed the debate on planning processes in general, the strong linkage with the object and the context distinguishes spatial planning processes from many other policy and administrative processes.

Next to location-specific objects and contexts of planning, **procedural aspects can also be locationally specific.** We argue that, in spatial planning, planning processes are tailored to specific spatial planning challenges. This chapter explores how both actors and procedural conditions shape planning processes and how their interrelation influences the development and outcome of such planning processes. This means that procedural conditions are shaped by the actors who participate in planning processes. Actors have certain goals and means at their disposal (such as money, power, instruments, or networks) to influence planning processes and their outcomes. So procedural conditions can – over time, through institutional reforms – also be shaped by actors.

At the same time, it should be noted that such processes are not unique to the domain or discipline of spatial planning. Planning processes also occur in other policy fields and in the business world, some of which can be rather strict and legalized (e.g., logistical processes at mainports such as Amsterdam Schiphol Airport). The **special position of processes in spatial planning** is due to their spatial and societal impacts. For instance, (re-)zoning of land can have severe implications for how and by whom certain sites or even parts of cities or regions are used.

DOI: 10.4324/9781003230489-3

This chapter explores the planning process as an **ideal-typical policy cycle** with its sub-phases (Section 3.1). Section 3.2 on actors and governance explores how spatial planning processes in practice often deviate from this sequential model under influence of interactions between actors in governance networks. This section is finalized by a discussion on integrated planning that explores the challenges of a governance approach in spatial planning and discusses recent trends in governance. The illustration of Dutch regional governance in Section 3.3 finally shows how governance plays out in spatial planning practice.

3.1 The process of planning as a policy cycle

In many definitions of spatial planning, there is an **explicit focus on the process** of planning. For instance, Nuissl and Heinrichs (2011) broadly understand spatial planning as "the process of decision making in a society on the use of land, based on assessing and balancing competing demands" (p. 47). These competing demands are acted out by different public and private stakeholders – such as citizens, landowners, sectoral planning authorities, etc. (Section 3.2). In this section, we will focus on the first part of this definition, that is, the process of decision making in a society. In public policy making, this process is structured into different phases. The plan preparation phase is particularly relevant for decision-making processes that involve the use of land. In spatial planning, we also refer to this plan preparation phase as the 'plan-making process'.

3.1.1 Different phases of the planning process

From a public policy perspective, different **phases of a public policy process** can be distinguished. Main phases include policy programming, policy implementation, and policy evaluation (Shahab *et al.* 2018; Knoepfel *et al.* 2011). While this characterization applies to spatial planning likewise, a more nuanced description of the policy cycle helps to better grasp the specifics of spatial planning as a public policy activity. An ideal-typical planning process can therefore be distinguished in the phases shown in Figure 3.1.

Phase 1: problem identification

At the start of each planning process usually stands the identification of the planning problem. The **planning problem provides legitimacy for the planning intervention**. It is thus essential to identify the

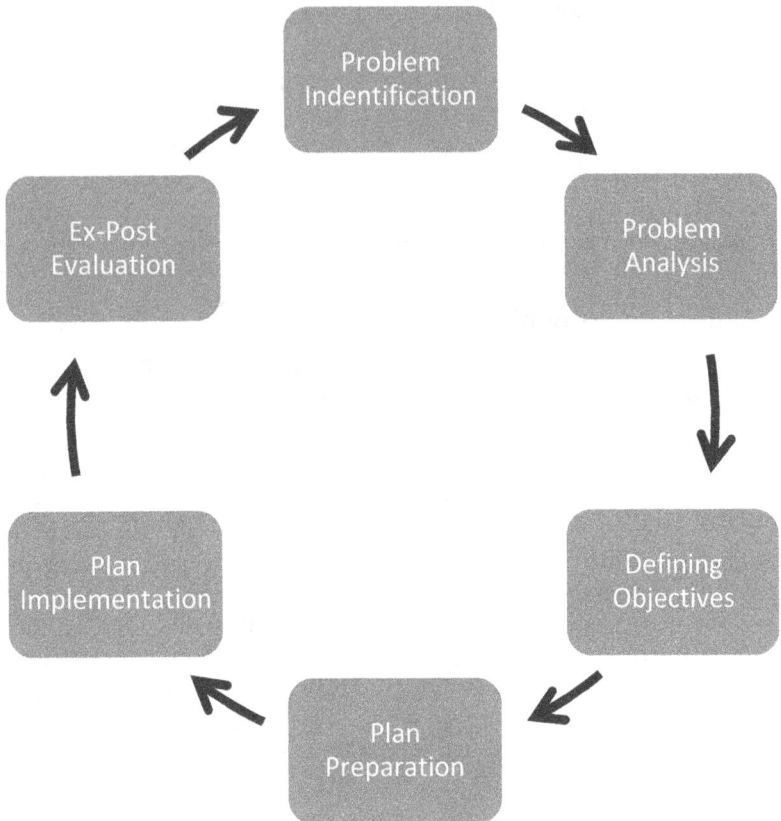

Figure 3.1 Policy cycle of spatial planning

planning problem not only very clearly, but also in a way that is publicly acceptable (as legitimacy can be conceived as the public acceptance of a policy intervention; Needham *et al.* 2018).

The spatial problem can be inherent to the planning object, such as an intensified land-use, for example, excessive densities that lead to tensions between residential land-use and other land-uses, or nuisances that create negative externalities (noise, air or visual pollution), but also scarcity of land for a certain purpose (nature, housing, infrastructure, etc.). A planning problem can emerge out of a dissatisfactory process – for example, because citizens are unhappy about the way a certain previous plan came about. A famous example is the

German project Stuttgart21, a procedural planning disaster of a station renewal (Selle 2010). The planning problem can also come from changing contexts, such as socio-economic dynamics, demographic changes, legal reforms, or changing environmental conditions.

What constitutes a planning problem is oftentimes not obvious at first sight. Even in situations where a clear causal relation between a polluter and a spatial pollution is identified, there are usually different interests and perspectives at stake. An example is the placement of a 'Locally Unwanted Land Use, LULU' (e.g., Davy 1997), like a waste incinerator facility, or an airport extension near a residential neighbourhood. The airport extension can be seen as a source of pollution (with the according 'Not In My Back Yard' NIMBYism responses), but it can also be seen as a benefit for a region (in the sense that it promises to provide labour and economic growth). Which perspective prevails is often a question not only of facts and figures regarding the issue at stake, but it is also a question of recognition of certain spatial claims. This was also illustrated by the example of the Betuweroute extension in the previous chapter. Spatial planning discriminates between often competing problem perceptions of actors. Which planning problems are recognized, and which not, and which of the recognized problems are left uncontrolled and which are pursued by planning initiatives is thus highly political and normative.

It can be argued that the problem identification is the most important phase of the planning process, as the political definition of the planning problem influences what is assumed to be the cause of the problem and thus influences the intervention strategy (Knoepfel *et al.* 2011). Rittel and Webber already pointed out in 1973 that planning problems are inherently wicked problems, and that oftentimes no simple answer can be found to resolve them. The multiple perspectives of different actors that assess a planning problem in different ways contribute to this wickedness. In other words, the problem identification is one of the first major challenges of the planning process.

Phase 2: problem analysis

Once the problem has been identified, the next phase attempts to analyze the problem. What components does the problem consist of and how can the relationships between them be valued? The problem analysis consists of a description of the current situation within an area, often per theme, based on existing sources (policy documents, secondary datasets, etc.). Such themes include public housing, demography, social aspects, public space, greenery, traffic and transport, facilities, quality of life, economy, employment, etc. The problem analysis is an important input for the following phases. The quality of the analysis thus also lays the foundation for the quality of the approach chosen and the potential solution to the problem.

In terms of public policy analysis, the analysis aims to identify the **causal relations** that lead to the problem. This causal relation can be formulated as a causal hypothesis (Knoepfel *et al.* 2011). It could be, for example, that shortage of housing is a planning problem of lacking availability of building land. Such a causal hypothesis will most likely lead to a planning strategy to designate more building land for the respective land-use. However, the causal hypothesis for the same problem could also be that the shortage of housing results from work-related migrations to the cities. Such an alternative causal hypothesis will lead to yet a different planning intervention (such as influencing the allocation of labour over a region or country).

Spatial planning aims to influence the behaviour of a certain target group of actors that is conceived to be at the root of the planning problem at stake (Gerber *et al.* 2018). If, for example, the availability of land is perceived as the causal hypothesis, the target group will be the landowners, developers, and municipalities, and their planning task then is to facilitate a quick production of housing. But if the migration is at the root of the problem, industry and employers become the focus for potential (spatial) solutions. The target group identified in the causal hypothesis during the problem analysis can solve the problem that is experienced by the owners of the planning problem as described in the previous phase of the policy cycle.

So, next to the problem identification (phase 1), the problem analysis (phase 2) also entails many elements that fundamentally change the way a planning process unfolds.

Phase 3: defining objectives

Based on the problem analysis, or the causal hypothesis, a so-called 'intervention hypothesis' is developed. The intervention hypothesis describes how "the collective problem requiring resolution can be mitigated and, indeed resolved by policy" (Knoepfel *et al.* 2011, p. 59). This is manifested in the defining of policy objectives. The resulting objectives in turn form input for the next phase in the planning process: the plan preparation phase. This step reflects in a hidden way the level of quality that is pursued with this planning problem. Implicitly or explicitly, this means that the level of ambition plays a role in setting the objectives.

It may not be underestimated how significantly the **preconditions of the planning processes** often determine the scope of the solutions. The preconditions mostly originate from the context (that is further discussed in the next chapter) and usually concern the possible use of resources (financial, legal, administrative, communicative), the runtime of the planning and implementation, the number of stakeholders, but also the political configuration of the responsible legal body (such as the city council), lobbyism, etc. All such aspects can influence the definition of policy objectives. The objectives are often formulated by actors other than the planning professional. In the transition from problem identification and problem analysis to plan preparation, the planner must make way for the political-administrative dimension in setting the objectives. Only after the objectives have been formulated (politically or administratively), the planner can start with the plan preparation.

Phase 4: plan preparation (the 'plan-making process')

A solution is created in the plan preparation phase. In the terminology of public policy, plan preparation is the phase of **policy formulation**. In spatial planning, this phase is also often referred to as the plan-making process. In this phase of the policy cycle, the instruments and procedures are defined to resolve the (spatial) problem under consideration. It is based on the results of the previous phases: the causal hypothesis and the intervention hypothesis regarding the identified problem (Knoepfel *et al.* 2011).

Sometimes during the preparation of a plan, **the planning process is aborted,** because for instance, the problem is no longer considered a problem (the problem identification changes), spatial planning as a domain is not the problem-owner of the specific problem (the causal hypothesis is reconsidered), a spatial plan is not considered the most effective or efficient solution for the problem (the intervention hypothesis is rejected), or the problem is not considered 'solvable' ('untameable' or wicked problems; Rittel and Webber 1973).

In the plan preparation phase, a **systematic consideration of locational requirements, space requirements and quality characteristics** lead to spatial sketches or designs and the actual plan design. The plan design (created through scenarios, sketches, visons, etc.) is a creative and value-bound process; it is therefore no more than a tool and not an end (Zoete 1997). Other assessment criteria may also play a role in the plan design, such as political or financial feasibility. After the plan design is finalized, the preferred alternative is chosen. The spatial planning process in terms of the plan design is now ready. After that, the plan has yet to be adopted. In order to also establish a legally binding land-use plan, a separate process is required with participation and consultation. Ultimately, this leads to the formal adoption of a plan. In practice, both facets occur simultaneously. Planners must therefore understand the spatial and legal process at the same time.

Though a binding land-use plan can be considered by default as the main planning instrument that is chosen, spatial planning can employ different **alternative forms of policy interventions** such as policy documents, spatial visions, sectoral or strategic plans or programmes. The form of the chosen solution depends on the problem and the associated objectives. Also, environmental or safety regulations can have a substantial impact on the selection of a planning intervention (Dembski 2020). However, it can be stated that the spatial plan is by and large still the most important type of policy intervention for spatial planning.

Spatial plans can differ considerably, for example in the level of detail or the way they are implemented (see phase 5). A plan can, for example, be rather open and leave a lot of scope for different land-uses, or it can be very detailed, specifically pre-determining which land-uses are allowed, and which are not. So, the degree of flexibility can differ (Van den Hoek *et al.* 2020). Which degree of flexibility is desirable for a specific situation differs per location and needs to be assessed on a case-by-case basis.

Phase 5: plan implementation

Once a plan, programme, policy document, etc., has been approved, the plan can be implemented. Although planning authorities have the formal responsibility of spatial planning, the implementation of planning interventions entails **many other public, private, and civil actors** (Needham 2014). This is further explored in the next section. Still, (formal) planning authorities play an important role in implementing plans, especially in the Netherlands. There are for instance different degrees to which a municipality can play either a more active or a more passive role in the plan implementation (e.g., Van Oosten *et al.* 2018).

In Dutch active land policy, planning authorities are traditionally more involved than in more passive systems, such as, for example, Germany (Hartmann and Spit 2015a). While in passive systems the planning authority provides the building rights, it does not usually directly implement the proposed changes in the built environment.

This is left to market actors who either do or do not pick up the development right. In countries with passive land policy, the implementation of spatial plans is a special problem with specific challenges, such as the building land paradox (Davy 1996). In contrast, in countries that practice active land policy, the implementation of plans is often already arranged in a (legal) contract between private developers and municipalities from the start. In fact, "de facto the majority of land-use plans showed more similarity with a contract in which informal agreements are formalized ex post" (Buitelaar 2012, p. 215). In active land policy, the planners – often together with private actors – must bring together resources (financial, regulative, etc.), actors and other process elements at the right time and in the right context.

So, to implement a spatial plan, the planning authority needs to choose **the appropriate strategy**. Whether a more facilitating (passive) approach makes sense, or an active land policy, or some form in between, depends on the object and the context. This is where the planning triangle can help to identify framework conditions for the implementation phase.

Phase 6: ex-post evaluation

Ex-post evaluation is mostly judgemental. An ex-post evaluation provides an explicit assessment of the effect of the process and the role of actors involved in this, but also of the outcomes of a plan. To understand ex-post plan evaluation, it is necessary to also understand **policy failures**. A policy failure can emerge because the plan could not be implemented as intended (failure of the intervention), or policy failures can mean that a plan does not achieve the desired effects (the causal hypothesis is inaccurate) (Patton and Sawicki 1986). Due to its judgemental and retrospective nature, this type of evaluation is not very popular and therefore often not systematically executed.

Answering the question of whether planning has been effective in **achieving its goals** requires not only a look at what has been realized and developed in the landscape, but also to look at what has not been built (Needham 2014). While the question of effectiveness is still relatively easy to answer – though it is not done regularly in practice (Spit and Zoete 2016), the question if planning was efficient is much more difficult to answer (Needham 2014).

In closing this list of phases, it is important to stress the relative importance of the order of this list. For the sake of convenience, they are presented here as a logical and recognizable list. However, there is a strong and continuous interaction between all phases. This will be further explained in the next section.

3.2 Actors and governance – towards open planning processes

Although the policy cycle as described in the previous section seems to provide a systematic planning procedure, in planning practice, such processes are often **very diverse and less cyclical in nature.** While the phases are presented here as logical steps and in a sequential order, in practice, these phases often run together and past each other, objectives and solutions are continually adjusted, and in between, formal or informal evaluations take place on an ongoing basis ('ex-ante evaluation'). Each planning process is therefore essentially a cyclical-iterative process: the same phase can be completed several times. So, the planning process is less clear than it appears on paper.

3.2.1 Actors interact in governance networks

Spatial planning needs to deal with this **messiness of planning processes.** Thereby, an important aspect of every plan-making process is to align the different components of such a process as to specifically relate to the actors, instruments, and means/assets involved, preferably by making use of a planning concept. This alignment between diverging components of a process is one of the most difficult tasks in spatial planning, both academically as well as practically. The role of actors is crucial in this process. The choice for the involvement and participation of certain actors has implicit or explicit consequences for the planning instruments and resources. It is therefore important for spatial planning to conduct a stakeholder analysis to understand the interest and influences (i.e., power) of different types of actors (Bryson 2004; Hermans and Thissen 2009).

The **distinction between actors** involved is important, because during the spatial planning process, it must be decided which actors will or will not be actively involved in the process. If the responsible government chooses to carry out the process as compactly as possible, it will be inclined to limit the number of actors as much as possible. Stakeholders will then only be involved in the process if formally required. However, if an open and interactive planning process has been chosen, then it is obvious that all those involved play a role in the process in one way or another. This has enormous consequences for the complexity (and thus for the manageability) of the process. It will be clear that these are two extremes. There is a lot of variation in the way in which actors are involved in a spatial planning process. However, with the selection of actors – given the identified problem and the broader societal context – and the way in which they are involved in the planning process, the main preconditions of the spatial planning process are established.

Bringing different stakeholders together in spatial planning links planning inextricably with **governance**. Ansell and Torfing (2016) define governance as "the interactive processes through which society and the economy are steered towards collectively negotiated objectives" (p. 4). This resembles the practical definition by Pierre (2005) who states that governance is "the process of coordinating and steering the urban society toward collectively defined goals" (p. 448). Although these working definitions contain the main elements of what governance is essentially about, when some more elaborate definitions are reviewed, it gives us a more precise understanding of the elements we will deal with in this chapter. For instance, in their handbook on the geographies of urban governance, Gupta *et al.* (2015) define governance as "the multiple ways through which city governments, businesses and residents interact in managing their urban space and life, nested within the context of other government levels and actors who are managing their space, resulting in a variety of urban governance configurations" (p. 4). In a similar vein, Healey (2006) stresses: "the extent to which the diverse actors and networks which coexist within a territory, urban region, city or neighbourhood cluster around a territorial focus, and create the capacity to act (collective actor capacity) for a territory" (p. 302).

In summary, in spatial planning, the process is of prime importance and links closely to many notions about governance. Governance deals with processes in which actors work together to achieve collectively defined goals. This does not mean that planning is inevitably consensus-oriented and interactive. Formally, planning processes also help to legitimize planning interventions against the **interests of some stakeholders**.

3.2.2 *Changing role of governance*

The method and phases of the planning process as described in Section 3.1 – which generally shape the structure of governance networks – are obviously ideal-typical and originate from the object-oriented planning tradition of blueprint planning. It has been described earlier how the evolution of planning thought in the Netherlands coincided with planning theoretical developments in the academic debate: from object-oriented blueprint planning towards a process-oriented 'communicative turn' and finally towards more context-oriented open planning approaches. In this section, we describe how these changes in planning theory and planning practice also implied **different orientations towards the role of actors in governance processes**. We first briefly describe the shift from blueprint planning to process planning, then the shift from process planning to open planning, and finally we elaborate on the role of actors in open planning processes.

Blueprint planning was characterized by the presentation of a final image or vision, which was expected to be executed automatically and thus become a reality. The various steps in the planning process as described earlier were completed chronologically, with 'the planner' – as an expert – being mainly in charge. However, planning practice soon showed that going through such steps in a linear fashion does not work. After all, in planning practice it turned out that in one phase the next phase is anticipated, while in the next phase there is continuous feedback to previous phases. Planning processes thus proceed much more iteratively than the phases sketched here suggest. During the 1960s, this became increasingly apparent.

Gradually, the realization became increasingly prominent that planning processes do not take place in a vacuum but are influenced by developments in society. During the 1970s and 1980s, planning was gradually no longer seen exclusively as a governmental task. With this change in thinking, space was created for third parties (e.g., private businesses, civil stakeholders) to participate in planning processes. This is amongst others illustrated by the clear rise of interest in public–private partnerships in this period (Van den Hof 2006). However, public–private partnerships tend to focus on the later stages in the planning process, especially the concrete plan preparation and plan implementation phases. This is mainly where private interests lie. As a result, the preliminary phases of most planning processes remained dominated by public parties.

In the pursuit of support for plan implementation and increasing the legitimacy of spatial planning processes and outcomes, many experiments were carried out in the 1990s with so-called '**open planning**'. This took shape in different ways and concepts (such as interactive policy making and interactive planning). In essence, it focuses on involving third parties (i.e., non-governmental stakeholders) in the planning process at the earliest possible stage. An essential point in this type of approach to spatial planning is the conviction that reality can be controlled by directly influencing the actors and not only through a formal plan (Boelens 2009). The latter no longer works in our society (as has been shown) and in many situations is no longer accepted in our society. And it is precisely in the direct contact – that is, in a strong connection with the actual decision-makers in the sectors, in the public debate and in offering the prospect of more desirable visions of the future – that the real strength of spatial planning ultimately lies (Zoete 1997).

An open planning process typically follows the general sequence as described in the policy cycle, but with some important deviations in which **the role of the third-party actors** is particularly stressed (see Zoete 1997 for a full elaboration). First, all actors are identified at an early stage and are already involved in the problem identification and problem analysis phases. Second, a public debate is organized before a draft plan is designed. This public debate can be for everyone (an "open evening") but is usually at first only organized for invited guests. For example, the group of non-selected actors can be initially addressed, but a broader representation of the actors already involved can also be useful, and finally all those who are involved in one way or another. Third, the formal legal preliminary consultation starts alongside the organization of the external communications. Examples are forms of participation and consultation with third parties as provided for in formal planning procedures.

It is thus typical of open planning processes that it is not only the government that makes the plan, but that it arises in the **interaction of the government and other actors**. The government does not work primarily through steering (acting based on legal power), but by developing governance networks (based on the ability to come to a joint plan with other authorities and private and civil partners, with commitment from all those involved). In this way, an open planning process can represent added value that is recognized by all parties involved. This added value is created by linking or coordinating interests, problems, and solutions. The term 'integration' is often used for this. In the next section, we will further delve into the term 'integration' while acknowledging that this not only applies to the process (governance), but also has clear links to the object and context of planning.

3.2.3 Governance and integrated planning

Policy integration is important at all levels of government. It is then obvious that spatial coordination should also take place within the planning system. This leads to a classic coordination problem of spatial planning. Traditionally, the planning system is based on a division of planning in relation to levels of government, which is organized as follows:

1. The national government makes long-term plans (>10 years) at the macro level (strategic planning).
2. The province or regional government then makes plans at the meso level (i.e., for the entire province or large parts thereof) for the medium term (5–10 years) (tactical planning).
3. The municipality makes concrete plans for the short term (2–5 years) at the micro level (operational planning).

The search for successful **forms of coordination** between all kinds of sectoral policy with spatial implications has always occupied a prominent place on the policy agenda of spatial planning. With the introduction of increasingly complex planning processes, the call for integration has grown stronger over the years. Policy integration is seen as a natural answer to complex planning problems. A clear example of policy integration is the increasing emphasis on sustainability, which calls for integrated attention to environmental (planet), economic (profit), and social (people) concerns. Campbell's (2016) sustainability triangle is a clear illustration of the coordination trade-offs that then occur between the different sectoral dimensions of such an integrated planning challenge.

Now **a dilemma arises**: in spatial planning, there is a growing need to increasingly coordinate, but at the same time it is becoming increasingly difficult to achieve the required level of coordination. After all, it is precisely because of the increased spatial dynamics that the need for further coordination and integration is continuously growing, especially at a regional scale. This development increases the desire for a further degree of integration in spatial planning. Complexity is increasing due to a changing society. In practice, the dilemma manifests itself in this way: on the one hand, a growing need for coordination, and on the other, this is becoming increasingly less fulfilled because of the problems in realizing and implementing integrated planning. A clear example of a complex, integrated planning challenge at the regional level in the Netherlands is the current discussion on the residential development of the Rijnenburg polder close to Utrecht. Here you see a clear need to balance different social (i.e., affordable housing, quality of life), economic (i.e., competitiveness of the Utrecht region, profitability of greenfield land development), and environmental (i.e., nature and landscape protection, fine dust emissions, etc.) interests.

The desire to achieve an increasingly better coordination of interests and solutions in spatial planning is an ambition to be appreciated. But this also entails at least **three pitfalls**, particularly at the regional scale and especially if we make integration (even if it is at a lower ambition level) a goal. First, the pursuit of integration in governance processes can provoke procrastination among participants. After all, with the argument of increasing support, decisions in coordination processes can be endlessly postponed. The argumentation remains legitimate, but the policy intentions seldom leave the paper and the consultation tables in the end. Second, in the end, hardly any distinction is made between important and less important dimensions of the problem (i.e., prioritization). The use of an integrated approach in coordination processes invites participation and suggests a certain (equal) contribution to everyone. This method often leads to disappointment and frustration. After all, the actual contribution is always reserved for the most important parties involved and it is usually (often forced by the preconditions) already outlined at an early stage. Third, the two pitfalls together offer opportunities to actors to block the process. The fact that quite a few conflicts of interest are crystallizing at the regional level feeds the notion that this last pitfall may well be the most important one, as will be shown by the example in the next section.

How do we get out of this outlined dilemma? **New forms of coordination** will have to be sought that do more justice to the nature of the problem and the position of the actors involved. Although coordination issues are increasingly leaving their mark on spatial planning problems, the pursuit of even more far-reaching forms of policy integration does not provide *a* solution, meaning *one* specific solution; rather, solution*s* (*plural*) must be sought and found in shared agreements about policy coordination. This aligns with the ideas of Scharpf (1997) about multilevel governance and has gained much response in academia over the years (e.g., Hooghe *et al.* 2001; Stephenson 2013).

In contemporary planning practice, the classical system as mentioned at the beginning of this section has in many cases been replaced (although not necessarily formally) by **a multilevel governance scheme**, in which the various authorities determine their own interests and development wishes, based on their position and the associated interests. In this, the nature of the problem determines the primary responsible actor, after which, in an open network and negotiation process, selective coordination is sought with other partners. It is obvious that this approach is not limited to public parties. Other non-governmental stakeholders (semi-public, private, and civil parties) can also play an important role.

The multi-level governance approach and its relation to integrated planning are further illustrated by zooming in on the Dutch case of regional governance in the next section. This example sketches both the advantages and the difficulties of multilevel, integrated governance approaches, especially in solving spatial planning problems at the regional level.

3.3 Example: Dutch regional governance

A clear example of the difficulty of effective and efficient multilevel, integrated governance approaches at the regional level is to be found in the Dutch case of regional governance (or rather: the lack thereof). This section first sketches the wider problem setting of the so-called 'institutional void' at the regional level, then outlines the complexity of regional planning challenges, and finally applies it to the difficult role of the provinces in Dutch regional governance practices.

3.3.1 Introducing the institutional void

The **governability of metropolitan regions** is a main theme in the governance literature (e.g., Innes *et al.* 2010; Mouat and Dodson 2013). Because of economic growth and globalization, many policy regions have expanded, leading to large cities 'swallowing' their immediate surroundings. This causes metropolitan authorities to re-border, both conceptually and pragmatically. The object of planning is shifting towards higher levels of scale, meaning that the attention of governance processes has often increased to the level of entire city-regions (e.g., Innes *et al.* 2010). In this respect, Hajer (2003) argues that when policy- and practical scales shift, policymaking often takes place in an 'institutional void', in which there are no accepted rules or norms regarding the course of action that is to be followed.

Spatial planning processes at this regional scale are thus often positioned in an institutional void, which is sometimes alternatively known as the '**regional gap**' (Van Straalen and Witte 2018). McGuirk (2008) realizes that institutional fragmentation is a key problem in this regional gap. The solution to this problem is to be found within the dimensions of the planning triangle. For instance, Hajer (2003), McGuirk (2008) and Evers and De Vries (2013) all propose an open governance solution to the institutional void. In other words, the classical, coordinating approaches are deemed less useful. The literature suggests some pragmatic, hands-on solutions to the regional gap, in which the actors themselves and the institutions that they can use play a more prominent role. Dore (2001) suggests stronger governmental institutions. Also, Mouat and Dodson (2013) suggest that inter-actor trust can be very instrumental in network governance. In general, consensus exists over the fact that regional governance requires tailor-made solutions. However, spatial planning practice showcases that this is easier said than done.

3.3.2 Complex regional planning challenges in the Netherlands

The importance of the **regional scale** in Dutch spatial planning is often underestimated, as the practical illustrations in the previous chapters have also shown. Numerous sectoral goals and planning tasks must be given a place in a country where virtually every square metre already has a formal land-use zoning. At the regional scale, planning tasks converge that on the one hand exceed the local level (micro, operational) and on the other hand are too specific to be tackled on the provincial (meso, tactical) or national (macro, strategic) scale. Moreover, these planning tasks are often 'wicked'; they typically do not adhere to administrative boundaries and are therefore difficult to solve at one dedicated scale level. Such complex, regional planning challenges are often about the integration of multiple sectoral concerns such as water, noise, climate, energy, air, wind, sun, nature, housing, and mobility. How can this be tackled in an open planning process or (multilevel) governance approach?

The Dutch government is currently busy implementing the new planning law: the **Environment and Spatial Planning Act** *(Omgevingswet)*. This new law prescribes an integrated approach to the physical environment. Under the new law, the government acts as one organizational body, meaning that the institutional/administrative boundaries of regions and municipalities should no longer matter. This can be seen as a direct response to the declining importance of the classical planning system as described earlier. At the same time, each tier of government still has its own formal planning tasks and responsibilities. Municipalities, provinces, and the national government will thus continue to work together. How then to solve complex planning challenges under the Environmental and Spatial Planning Act? How to work together across administrative boundaries? Planning tasks continue to be relevant at various scale levels; how to deal with this? The new act is supposed to become a coherent institutionalized system of vision development, policy development, and implementation that will be instrumental in this.

Within this new institutionalized system, the **regions will play a key role**. This is stressed in the draft text of the NOVI (*Nationale Omgevingsvisie*; National Environmental Vision), which states that many choices for the physical environment must be considered at the level of the regions. The report states that: "because the responsibility for environmental policy largely rests with provinces, municipalities and water boards, in many cases substantive choices can best be made regionally" (*authors' translation*). The Environmental and Spatial Planning Act thus requires a lot of cooperation between all actors involved. This not only concerns the public sector but also requires cooperation from companies, social organizations, knowledge institutions, and residents. There is a tension here, because governments have formal responsibilities and powers and are political-administrative organizations with a legally binding responsibility to achieve set goals. The other actors involved obviously do not have the same position; they work from open, informal, and collaborative governance networks. There is a difference between these formal responsibilities of governments (as a public body with certain mandates) and the intention of governments (as 'equal partner') to work together with other actors in a network and thus to work together on a task in a project in a more informal way (Van Straalen and Witte 2018). This tension becomes clear when looking at the role of provinces in regional governance.

3.3.3 Dutch provinces in regional governance: learning by doing

Provinces can play an important role in finding solutions for complex spatial issues at the regional level. The provincial level in the Netherlands has traditionally been a hierarchical governmental institution, based on formal laws and regulations. More interesting, however, is the way in which provinces are trying to increasingly function as an equal partner in a much larger network under the institutional framework of the new Environment and Spatial Planning Act (Paris 2018). How can provinces become more involved in informal networks to be able to contribute to solving complex tasks from their formal role and powers?

Provinces advocate regional interest. They can usually better oversee the inter-municipal scale at which municipalities, companies, and other organizations work together. This allows provinces to help realize matching opportunities for specific local or sectoral subtasks. When provinces are able to coordinate informal cooperation at the regional scale, a much larger network can be included. As a result, larger regional projects can be set up, based on an informal governance approach. In this way, the 'tailor-made solutions' as mentioned before can be better delivered, without losing sight of the larger strategic purposes of provincial involvement in regional planning issues. This also provides a basis for making decisions about planning tasks at the regional level, in which provinces can take up a more leading role.

Several tools and strategies of open planning as have been discussed in this chapter can be instrumental to support such **regional governance processes**. First, by conducting research by design, the impact of the planning task in an area can be displayed on a map and thus clarified. Designing thus becomes more important in the process of vision formation, policy development and implementation. Second, in governance networks, it is important to express ambitions, to share interests and to continuously have good conversations with each other. By coupling knowledge, the planning task can be viewed from different perspectives. Making choices at the regional level is facilitated when the actors involved have the same knowledge and information. An independent process manager (i.e., a planner) can ensure that the process runs smoothly and can identify conflicts between actors and possible sources of stagnation. This helps to combat the pitfalls mentioned before. Third, learning by doing is an important aspect in collaborative processes at the regional scale. Accepting that the planning process is often a search process can be a first step. It is necessary to consider reflection and evaluation of and by those involved in the process (i.e., the cyclical-iterative nature of open planning processes). This makes it possible to respond in time to changes in society.

In summary, learning by doing, research by design, collaboration, and working at different levels of scale and based on formal powers can offer opportunities for regional collaboration under the Environmental and Spatial Planning Act in the Netherlands.

3.4 Discussion: the role of the planner in a governance setting

After outlining the evolution of planning thought and planning practice in Chapter 1 and pointing out the increasing normativity of the object of planning (Chapter 2) it is not surprising that in responding to this, the **process of planning is also getting increasingly complex**. This development has enormous consequences for the course of the planning process: the complexity of the collaborating parties (both public and private) is growing to immense proportions. The question arises how planning processes remain manageable. This requires new insights, in combination with different rules and adjusted institutional arrangements. Due to the changes in the societal and institutional contexts (Chapter 4), important shifts in emphasis have taken place in the rules of the game between the public actors involved. These are sometimes referred to in the literature as a shift from government to governance (Rhodes 2007).

The **transition from government to governance** has had major consequences for the way planning processes are organized. These became much more complex than in the blueprint and procedural planning periods (1960s and 1970s) and the existing laws and regulations were put into a different perspective. This means that the legislation and regulations are only implemented when the important matters have already been informally agreed upon. The working method within planning processes has thus shifted drastically, towards more communicative (1980s) and open (1990s–now) planning processes. Kreukels (1997) stated over two decades ago: the classical planning system has been abandoned. No longer is one actor (the national government) exclusively responsible for strategic planning (long term) and another (province) for tactical planning (medium term), and a third (municipality) for operational planning (short term). Currently, all levels of government work with all these different types of planning. In fact, private developers also display the same behaviour. For the chronology of planning processes, this means that various processes (public and private) with different planning horizons (short, medium, or long term) overlap at the same time. These processes are simultaneously operationally supported by projects that implement different components of the process. For planners, this means that they are increasingly expected to contribute their knowledge of the plan implementation to the plan preparation phase to provide spatial planning with a higher degree of reality.

At the same time, planners are increasingly **called upon as process managers**. This is due to the long lead time in planning processes. The planner is thus increasingly becoming a professional with his own substantive expertise that is combined with a generalist view of the spatial and administrative-legal environment in which spatial planning takes place. Thus, planners are increasingly shedding the somewhat boring stereotyped image of 'the planner' and are increasingly profiling themselves in the market as widely deployable generalists with their own substantive expertise. The work for planners in practice (as municipal officer, commercial consultant, etc.) has thus become more diversified – and, some say, more exciting. A similar development applies to spatial planning as an academic discipline. The need for reflection on the practice of spatial planning is growing. Both governments and the business community attach great value to good relations with universities. In this respect, spatial planning in academia and in planning practice mutually depend on each other.

3.5 Conclusion: increasing normativity

Planning processes mark the route to (re)design the built environment. Although this route is systematic, there are many roads that can lead to a plan. The **process is cyclical and iterative.** Some steps are (briefly) repeated, for example when a new stakeholder is invited to actively participate during the planning process. Cyclical-iterative also means anticipating what is to come and at the same time feeding back to previous steps. In this, the participants (the actors) all have their own interests and resources (such as knowledge, money, instruments, or networks) and, above all, this makes every planning process and every governance network essentially and per definition unique. Contrary to what is often assumed about spatial planning, many plans have no fixed (legal) procedures and even if so, large parts of the process are not very strongly legally anchored. The selection of actors – also in the informal circuit – is therefore of great importance for the success of planning processes.

Of course, careful planning of a process does not only occur in spatial planning, but in the whole of society. In spatial planning, planning processes typically stop with the actual plan as the end product, and not with its realization. As a result, the *process* of evaluating (this is also called 'ex-ante evaluation') plays an important role in the planning process itself.

After the phases of blueprint planning and procedural planning, a lot of attention is now afforded to open planning processes, which are often taken up in the wider discussion about the role of governance in planning. In blueprint planning, the expertise of the planner was very important. In procedural planning, much emphasis was placed on the (formal) process and less on the qualities of the actors and of the proposed spatial solution. The core idea of the open planning (governance) process is to **involve the relevant actors at the rights stage of the planning process.** And if the government really acts as an equal partner, this type of process puts the formal and traditional planning system into perspective even more, but at the same time brings to the fore the issue of normativity. From this point-of-view, spatial planning practice can be perceived to be quite remote from the formal, more legal system. There is thus a paradox between the strongly legally coloured planning system and the practice of spatial planning, which can also be very much dominated by the eye of the beholder.

4   The context of planning
An administrative and institutional context

Planning does not take place in a vacuum. Whether planning achieves the desired outcomes or not depends largely on the context in which it is planned. In some disciplines, like administrative science or business management, concepts can be transplanted and replicated elsewhere (e.g., certain forms of bookkeeping or human resource strategies). Planning, however, is not isotopic but rather **idiosyncratic** in the sense that it is location-specific and also time-sensitive. The location-specific characteristic follows from the characteristic of land as a – quite literal – fundamental basis of planning activity. Location is a unique and immovable feature of land, as has been discussed. Nevertheless, the image of the Netherlands, especially from an international perspective, is that most towns and cities look very similar to each other. Even this seemingly uniform functional and aesthetical spatial layout of Dutch cities can be explained on the basis of context variables, as will be shown in this chapter.

So, in different locations, the context of the land is different: environmentally, societally, politically, economically, etc. In addition, **context is also not static, but dynamic in time**. A plan that works in one period of time is likely to fail in other periods of time and vice versa. This has close links to the 'how' and 'by whom' questions that were addressed before. Planning is thus dependent on time and location characteristics. In this sense, spatial planning is "a child of its time" that mirrors societal developments (Kreukels 1985). Providing a comprehensive list of context variables relevant for spatial planning is, however, close to impossible. However, since we have defined spatial planning as a deliberate governmental activity aimed at intervening in society, it is very important to explicitly discuss both the administrative environment of the public sector as well as the societal context in which planning takes place. It could thus be stated that context refers

DOI: 10.4324/9781003230489-4

both to the specific administrative context (Section 4.1) and institutional setting (i.e., the planning system) (Section 4.2) in which planning activities are embedded, but also to the wider societal context in which planning occurs (Section 4.3). This chapter thus focuses on the administrative, institutional, and societal context variables related to the object of planning and the process of planning.

4.1 The administrative context of planning

As part of the executive branch of the state in the trias politica, spatial planning as public activity takes place in an administrative context. It determines the way in which spatial problems can be tackled. The administrative context in the Netherlands is central to this section. The administrative context can be described along some **key principles**, inherent to the system. One of the key principles of the Dutch administrative context, the 'equivalence principle', provides an important explanatory framework for the uniformity of spatial developments in the Netherlands. Spatial equality has also been the leading distribution mechanism for a long time in the relationship between the central (national) government and Dutch municipalities.

4.1.1 Allocation and equivalence: the third aspiration level of Goedhart

A systematic explanation of the influence of the administrative context on planning processes requires giving attention to structural tasks and relationships in the total system of public administration. This system is mainly determined by the legal system and financial flows. In turn, the system itself is based on a number of fundamental considerations about the tasks of the (national) government. **Two important mechanisms** in this respect are allocation and equivalence. In the *allocation* (distribution) of government funds, it appears that the so-called 'third level of aspiration' from the doctrine of Goedhart (Goedhart 1982) is very important. This third level strives for equality of local and regional facilities. This doctrine was developed in the 1950s and has ever since implicitly and explicitly functioned as the guiding principle behind most important spatial allocation issues in the Netherlands. The spatial effects of this are enormous – certainly after many decades. Not only has it affected the distribution of facilities across the Netherlands, but it has also served as a basic idea for distribution issues in Dutch society in general.

Goedhart's doctrine consists of **four levels of aspiration**. These levels not only describe the rationale of the financial organization of public administration, but also set certain standards for municipalities. In addition to these four levels, there is another level: it assumes fully autonomous municipalities where mutual differences are accepted. This could be characterized here as the 'base level'. In that sense, there are actually five levels of aspiration. Nonetheless, the four commonly accepted levels of the doctrine of Goedhart are explained in the following sections.

First aspiration level

The first aspiration level aims to **reduce excessive inequalities** in the so-called load capacity or carrying capacity of municipalities. If the differences in carrying capacities between municipalities are too great, a form of compensation must be found. Without compensation, a mechanism would be created whereby rich municipalities would become increasingly rich more quickly and poor municipalities would become increasingly poor (this is in a wider context also known as the 'Matthew-effect'; Rigney 2010). This effect of increasing inequality was soon considered undesirable in the administrative context of the Netherlands. That is why this first level already appeared in the second half of the 19th century. Before that, people only were familiar with the 'night watchman state' (this is the aforementioned 'base level'), in which the government only intervenes if absolutely justified.

Second aspiration level

On top of the aforementioned 'carrying capacity', the second aspiration level aims to also **reduce excessive inequalities** in the 'provision capacity'. Not only differences in carrying capacity are now visible, but also differences in basic needs and facilities of municipalities. In practice, this means that national governmental money will be made available for the basic provisions deemed necessary for all municipalities. This was the main governmental aim in the Netherlands directly following World War II. Spatially and functionally, this implies that whether a city fulfils a regional function depends entirely on the wider regional structure. If there is no other city in the region with such a package of inter-local facilities, this centre or nodal function means extra burdens for the municipal council. Additional resources are provided to compensate for an excessive backlog. This is an example that fits Goedhart's second level of aspiration.

Third aspiration level

The third aspiration level tries to achieve an **equal distribution of facilities** as much as possible. What is special is that the aim is not equality (the same everywhere) but equivalence. The ambition is a complete equalization of facilities. However, different gradations are possible within this pursuit of equality. The third aspiration level in the Netherlands expresses the ambition for each allocation issue. The consistent application of this level of ambition has had fundamental consequences for the spatial organization of the Netherlands. At the same time, it provides an explanatory framework for the spatial design of the Netherlands, an answer to the question. 'Why are cities and towns in the Netherlands all so similar?' This third aspiration level is in line with the idea of the welfare state, because, for example, all centres in a municipality receive equal facilities.

Fourth aspiration level

Goedhart's doctrine also mentions a fourth aspiration level. This fourth level is based on a **striving for real equality of provisions for municipalities**. Achieving such equality requires a very centralistic approach. This results in an outspoken paternalistic model with a strict central direction by the national government. This level completely clashes with the ambition of municipal autonomy (and the principle of subsidiarity), which has always been an important starting point in the organization of Dutch public administration. For this reason, this aspiration level is almost purely hypothetical. It requires a completely different structure in public administration, comparable to the centrally planned economies in the former communist countries in eastern Europe in the past century.

The use of the third aspiration level is of great importance in the distribution of resources by the national government and in the ministerial allocation of resources via sectoral policy. An important observation is that the equivalence principle has had major effects on the spatial planning of the Netherlands. Because this principle plays a major role in all policy sectors, comparable facilities have been realized throughout the Netherlands. This applies in the field of educational facilities, health care, welfare, social security, etc. The materialization of this is clearly visible. Everywhere in the Netherlands we find the same types of school buildings, hospitals, and roundabouts. This has had major advantages: it is recognizable and, in general, easier to use. Yet, this also has significant drawbacks related to effectiveness and efficiency. Not every standard facility is the optimal facility in the relevant municipality or region as, oftentimes, specific (i.e., contextual) needs, problems, or cultural aspects would make a different design more effective and efficient. Here we are in the middle of the tension between the allocation of wealth in the Netherlands and the tension between centralized and decentralized management in addressing spatial planning issues. Many problems and challenges crystallize in this field of tension, as the remainder of this chapter will show.

4.1.2 Financial flows and the principle of subsidiarity

The aim of this section is to clarify why the administrative context of spatial planning matters, what the **financial relationships** are, why the latter exist, how they work, and what their spatial effects are. In fact, it is about the old Dutch saying, 'Who pays, decides' (or, in other words, 'follow the money'). The financial flows from central government to the provinces and municipalities are therefore an important control instrument for the central government.

Two choices determine the distribution of financial resources. First comes the before-mentioned 'equivalence principle': the pursuit of equality (egalitarianism) between and within municipalities. Equality is experienced as justice. This means that many municipalities have comparable facilities but also that even the centres or districts within one municipality have equivalent facilities. The second principle is the subsidiarity principle: everything the 'lower' level of government can do, it also must do. As a principle, it has taken on the meaning that only in those cases where a problem transcends the level of the public authority involved, a higher authority takes its place. In other words, all resources and powers are, in principle, decentralized as far as possible (that is, to the administrative level of the municipality). One of the interesting questions in anticipating the new Environment and Spatial Planning Act is to what extent the principle of subsidiarity will be extended to also include the citizen as 'lowest' level of public administration. In other words, perhaps the new motto will be: what can be self-organized by civil society should also be self-organized.

In 1848, the Dutch statesman **Thorbecke** introduced **political principles** for the Netherlands that have been in place until today. Since then, the Netherlands has been a decentralized unitary state. This means, among other things, that not everything is arranged centrally, but that local authorities are partly autonomous or self-determined. But the principle of equality actually requires a strong grasp of higher authorities. And this again is at odds with the principle of subsidiarity.

What is regulated centrally, the central government directs with so-called 'golden cords': the municipalities 'in co-administration' must allocate certain money for specific matters. A government's 'room to manoeuvre' is determined by the financial space of a governmental body. That is why the financial relations are so important for understanding the context. The financial relations system was of great importance in the transition to the current welfare state. During that transition, the choice was made for centralization: the national government would collect and distribute the money. In consequence, for an average Dutch municipality, most of the municipal budget – about two-thirds of it – is derived from national allocation of money (Götze 2021).

The influence of the **financial relations between the three layers of government** is reflected in the spatial planning of the Netherlands. Developments in financial relations mean that local authorities are increasingly made responsible for the consequences of their administrative-political decisions. Budgets and tasks linked to them are becoming increasingly decentralized. This creates more policy freedom and autonomy for local authorities. However, the more autonomous action of municipalities is at odds with the principle of uniformity. After all, allowing more autonomy will most likely result in greater inequality between municipalities and this is not always politically desirable. The balance is constantly changing due to changing ideas of society, as also the following illustration on allocation issues and regional policy will show.

4.1.3 Dutch example: allocation issues and regional policy

In many countries, **regional planning exists at an intermediate level** between national and local levels, such as in Germany, the Netherlands, or France. Oftentimes, national and regional authorities are relatively weak in implementing spatial plans (Schmitt and Smas 2021), while municipalities hold the power to release binding land-use plans (Janssen-Jansen and Tan 2018). In the Netherlands, regional planning at the level of the 12 provinces has been subject to changes due to political dynamics, even though Dutch regional planning was traditionally strong (Van Straalen *et al.* 2014). In its origin, regional policies emerged out of the recognition of large regional disparities that were considered unacceptable in the light of the previous discussion on allocation, equivalence, and Goedhart's third aspiration level, which was meant to purposefully reduce inequality in regional service provision to a minimum.

The **importance of the regional level is gradually changing in the Netherlands,** as the discussion on regional governance in the previous chapter already highlighted. Two mutually reinforcing processes foster this development. First, even though a top-down distribution and decentralization of national governmental tasks is still happening, the formal position of the provinces as an administrative intermediate level of government is becoming less prominent. Second, there is a bottom-up phenomenon: some tasks exceed the problem space of municipalities and require regional cooperation (Wegener 2012), both in terms of the execution of those tasks and in terms of strategic policy. As a result, we see that the importance of the region as a spatial unit (i.e., the inter-municipal level) is increasing. We currently see both processes (top-down and bottom-up) happening simultaneously. On the one hand, the national government, in their strategic White Paper on the future spatial development of the Netherlands, called the National Environmental Vision (*Nationale Omgevingsvisie*), pinpoints 'daily urban systems' that can take up tasks at the regional level. On the other hand, municipalities are looking for organizational power at a higher level for planning issues that transcend the local level, such as the energy transition. The Regional Energy Strategies are an example of a new organizational layer at the regional (inter-municipal) level that is designed to collaboratively take up the energy transition challenges (Koelman *et al.* 2021).

These developments strengthen the **importance of the regional level,** but at the same time highlight the occurrence of the regional problem that was introduced before, the so-called 'regional gap' or 'institutional void' (e.g., Lester and Reckhow 2013). This means that, in practice, the formal governmental entity in charge of the intermediate administrative level – the provinces – is too big (spatially and functionally) to efficiently and effectively accept the responsibility for solving regional planning problems. At the same time, the regional spatial problems often are too complex to be solved by municipalities themselves, so a degree of regional coordination is desirable to tackle the problems. As a result, regional coordination challenges occur, both in terms of fragmentation of tasks and powers and in terms of legitimacy and/or democratic accountability of planning outcomes (e.g., Nuisll and Heinrichs 2011; Schmitt and Wiechmann 2018).

Various solutions have been devised for this in practice. These solutions consist of entering into partnerships (i.e., governance arrangements), making use of the existing administrative system through adjustments (fewer municipalities or more provinces), or by changing the existing system (by creating a fourth administrative layer).

Although various solutions have been debated in Dutch spatial planning for over four decades, only the merging of municipalities has been achieved as an effective response. So far, attempts to either merge the provinces into 'super-provinces' (e.g., 'Greater Amsterdam Metropolitan Area', Lambregts *et al.* 2008) or to organize a formal fourth level of administration at the regional scale have not led to a solid planning response to regional dynamics.

In the end, **cooperation at the regional level remains a necessity** to address planning problems, because many spatial developments do not stop at the municipal boundary. Think for instance of the construction of residential areas, business parks, green areas, transport infrastructures, etc. It is therefore of importance to guarantee administrative strength, continuity, and coherence in regional policies. Especially in urban areas, where the accumulation of the spatial tasks is most visible (work, housing, facilities, quality of life, environment) and the scarcity of physical space is the greatest, these kinds of matters are important and urgent. A clear example of this is the regional governance of the Randstad and Green Heart area in the Netherlands (e.g., Lambregts *et al.* 2008).

4.2 The institutional setting of planning: the formal planning system

The administrative context as described in the previous section is dependent on **legal frameworks and financial flows**. This section shows that the institutional context of spatial planning in reality takes a different position. In this section, we further elaborate on the significance of the formal planning system for the institutional context of spatial planning. In this, the main focus is on shifts within the planning system and the effect of national policy on municipal policy. This can be seen as a further elaboration on the tension between central and decentralized control as discussed in the previous section.

4.2.1 Functions and tensions of the planning system

Following de Ridder and Schut (1995), we **define the spatial planning system** as follows: the spatial planning system is a management structure for organized spatial decision-making on several levels of government, consisting of bodies, powers, instruments, and procedures. This spatial planning system is institutionalized in planning laws (Needham *et al.* 2018). It is important to realize that the existing planning system is not a tangible structure, but a thought construction in the minds of those involved, which is reflected in (legal and non-legal) rules. The design of the planning system is determined by the organizations that are part of it and by the rules of the game for the interaction between those organizations. The spatial planning system is thus based on assumptions about the best way to achieve spatial policy through a formal distribution of responsibilities for the different tiers of government.

Despite its formalized nature, the **practice of spatial planning** is characterized by **increasing dynamics and complexity**. Due to the increasing mobility of citizens and businesses, the dependencies between municipalities and provinces have grown (Lambregts *et al.* 2008; Wegener 2012). This development places high demands of flexibility on the spatial planning system, which is, however, focused largely on legal certainty, stability, and control to facilitate a steady growth. The result is that, for some spatial development projects, important spatial considerations have sometimes been made outside of the formal framework of the spatial planning system. Examples include major infrastructural works, such as the dedicated rail freight corridor from the Port of Rotterdam to the German hinterland (the Betuweroute) and the High-Speed Rail corridor from Amsterdam to Brussels (the HSL South). Apart from these exceptions, the overall performance (i.e., the effect) of national governmental spatial policy is in practice rather limited.

4.2.2 Balancing tensions in planning

Spatial planning needs to balance different spatial interests when deciding on the allocation and distribution of spatial resources. When weighting the different interests, there are fields of tension where spatial planning – implicitly or explicitly – positions itself. We here distinguish **five fields of tension** based on de Ridder and Koeman (1999, pp. 4–7), who distinguished tensions based on the (external) relationships between government and citizens and based on the (internal) relationships between governments.

Flexibility versus legal certainty

Since most plans, projects, and policy proposals have a long preparation time, they must be adaptable to changing societal, economic, or environmental circumstances (Hartmann and Needham 2012). Flexibility, on the one hand, is important in spatial planning to be able to adapt to changes. **Legal certainty**, on the other hand, is also important because it forms the basis for the rights of stakeholders (Bromley 2000). Legal certainty and its legal protection provide the basis for economic growth and interests, as it allows future-oriented investments and financial reliability. Legal certainty of planning and property rights entails an economic function for society (Van Straalen *et al.* 2018). Flexibility and legal certainty thus serve different interests in a planning process and are often at odds. Planning theory "ascertains the structural tension between flexibility and robustness as an important paradox of land use planning" (Van Straalen *et al.* 2018, p. 4). That is why we speak of a field of tension here. This tension is very prominent in spatial planning and can be illustrated with different lock-in situations (see examples in Hartmann and Needham 2012). A further distinction can be made in material and procedural flexibility, and even within planning instruments, such as binding land-use plans, planners have some scope of discretion in the flexibility (Van den Hoek *et al.* 2020). In the face of major changes and uncertainties, planning theory suggests evading the tension of flexibility and robustness (i.e., legal certainty) with concepts such as resilience, adaptation, or evolutionary planning (Van Straalen *et al.* 2018, p. 4). However, the basic tension remains, and planners need to position planning decisions in the pendulum swing of flexibility and legal certainty.

Property rights versus public policy regulation

This area of tension concerns the fundamental question to what extent a government may infringe upon property rights for a redevelopment of space it advocates. Property rights are considered robust institutions (Van Straalen *et al.* 2018). Property rights are embedded in the Universal Declaration of Human Rights (Article 17) and warranted by the European Convention of Human Rights (Article 1, Protocol No. 1). However, property does not provide unlimited freedom, rather public policy can regulate the way the right to property in land can be exercised (Needham *et al.* 2018). As land is a scarce resource (Hartmann and Gerber 2018), it seems legitimate to intervene in its allocation and distribution. One of the constraints, however, is the **principle of proportionality**, which is one of the key principles of governmental action (Needham *et al.* 2018). It entails that any governmental intervention needs to withstand a test that proves an intervention as 'appropriate, necessary, and suitable' to achieve the desired policy outcome (Ellis 1999). 'Appropriate' means that the costs and the impact of an intervention may not exceed the benefits of an intervention; 'necessary' means that no softer intervention can achieve the goal; 'suitable' means that the intervention is actually able to achieve the goal; a causal relation must exist between the intervention and the result it achieves. So, public policy faces strong restrictions when intervening in property rights, due to its strong constitutional protection (Tarlock and Albrecht 2016). Due to this notion, planning via public policy is often conceived as weak against private property (Gerber *et al.* 2018). However, interventions in property rights are essentially part of spatial planning. Spatial planning needs to carefully design interventions in property rights. Notwithstanding the normative stance in this debate, planning needs to carefully design policy interventions that strike a balance between property rights interventions and public policy regulations. The legal system – with the principle of proportionality and other legal principles – sets the frame for balancing property and its regulation.

Decisiveness and expertise versus participation and stakeholder involvement

Ever since Arnstein's 'ladder of citizen participation' (Arnstein 1969), spatial planners debate on the merits and pitfalls of **participation**. On the one hand, extensive participation procedures and legal procedures for stakeholders tend to slow down the decision-making process (Selle 2010), which can put the decisiveness of spatial policy under severe pressure. On the other hand, participation, and stakeholder involvement can play a crucial role in implementing spatial planning. While certain participation and stakeholder involvement is prescribed in planning law – usually an early-stage participation and a plan display at the final stage (Hartmann *et al.* 2018) – planners have a vast range of possibilities and scope when it comes to participation. Proponents of strong participation use arguments such as the increased legitimacy, democratic quality, plan quality, and level of information to citizens (Hartmann *et al.* 2018), some celebrating participation and collaboration as a panacea (Silver *et al.* 2010; Healey 1996; Edelenbos 2000). On the other hand, critical voices point out that, in planning practice, it has merely become "ritual dances" and "window dressing" (Wolsink 2003; Edelenbos 2000). Allmendinger and Haughton (2010) see the irony that the striving for consensus in planning via participation and collaboration leads to opposition, which can ultimately even undermine the legitimacy of a planning effort. Planning by expertise versus planning via participation represents different forms of legitimacy (Hartmann and Spit 2016). Finding the right balance can be difficult and forms a tension between decisiveness and expertise on the one hand and participation and stakeholder involvement on the other hand. This challenge is also influenced by contextual factors, such as changing public opinions, but also technological developments, giving rise to, amongst others, e-participation (Donders *et al.* 2014; Jiang 2019).

Central versus decentral

A constant source of tension lies in **the relationships between the various governmental authorities.** As the spatial policy of the provinces and central government began to become more important, increasingly conflicts arose about the question of which government layer has primacy in addressing concrete planning problems. Although the subsidiarity principle is in place, a clear demarcation of responsibilities between government layers remains elusive. The new Environmental and Spatial Planning Act foresees coordination of three governmental layers in spatial planning: the national government, the regional level (provinces), and municipalities. In many policy fields, the national government formulated strategic policy for the longer term, the province pursued a policy for the medium term within it, and the municipality had an operational policy within the given frameworks. But in spatial planning, substantive policy of the national government is almost entirely indicative. This means the policy should usually only be "taken into account in all reasonableness" in (spatial) decisions at the regional and municipal level.

Comprehensive versus sectoral planning

A final source of tension in planning stems from the **difference between comprehensive and sectoral planning.** In line with the earlier distinction made between sectoral planning and comprehensive planning in Chapter 1, Derksen (1994) once strikingly remarked that "spatial planning never became what it should have been: a comprehensive policy in which the interests of all sectors would be carefully weighed against each other" (p. 4). Even though this statement was made almost three decades ago, it has remained relevant over the years within the planning debate. The self-evident efficiency of sector-based planning versus the sector-transcendent benefits of integrated planning has been repeatedly discussed by various planning scholars (Spit 1998; Janssen-Jansen 2004; Van Ark 2005; Waterhout 2007; Vigar 2009; Witte and Spit 2014; Suprayoga *et al.* 2020a). Also, its relevance remains visible today as is, for instance, illustrated in the recent discussions on the role of integrated planning in the Environment and Spatial Planning Act. The fact that this ambition of integration could never be fully realized by comprehensive planning has challenged other sectoral departments to fill this gap. Some departments have made vigorous use of this. For example, in the field of the environment and in the field of nature and landscape protection, parallel decision-making circuits have developed.

The five fields of tensions in planning illustrate how spatial planning is always a balancing act. But also, the weighting of tensions is to a large extent dependent on the locational-specifics and the tensions are not static. So, a one-size-fits-all answer to how to deal with the tensions cannot be determined. This raises the question of the freedom of action of spatial planning. This issue will be addressed in the next section.

4.2.3 *Dynamics and performance of planning*

The answer to the question whether and to what extent freedom of action exists in spatial policy at the municipal level is important for spatial planning. Is this directly controlled through national or provincial policies or is there a clear freedom of action within formulated margins ('setting the framework')? A fundamental issue in spatial planning is the question at **what level of government** the centre of gravity of spatial management should lie. The normativity of this question becomes obvious when recognizing that some planners believe the central government should be more directive and municipalities should not be entrusted with all spatial issues, due to the self-interests of municipalities in certain issues (Wegener 2012; Lambregts *et al.* 2008), while others believe that the central government should only determine the general frameworks and that municipalities (and market parties, or citizens) in particular should determine spatial developments (in line with the principle of subsidiarity). It should be noted here that (national) governmental policy can manifest itself in various ways, such as in plans, projects, subsidies, memoranda, or studies.

In this context, it is relevant to look at **policy implementation**. Policy implementation describes a "set of processes after the programming phase that are aimed at the concrete realisation of the objectives of a public policy" (Knoepfel *et al.* 2011, p. 206). Policy does not implement itself. Implementation theory in policy studies therefore explores how, why, and by whom policy is realized (Schofield 2001). Classical policy implementation approaches assess the deficits between the current state of a system and a desired state (i.e., the policy objective). The difference is the policy implementation, and it can be assessed as 'achieved' or as 'failed'. This way of measuring policy implementation can be understood as performance or conformance (De Lange *et al.* 1997). The merits of evaluating policy implementation with the criterion of performance or conformance are that it establishes a link between policy and its execution, which in turn increases justification for interventions. Also, it provides credibility and accountability, as the success and failure are clearly connectable (Shahab *et al.* 2019).

We define performance here as – literally or otherwise – implementing/executing spatial policy in the top-down line, from central government to the provinces and then to the municipalities. If there is influence of government policy in the field of spatial planning on the policy of other governmental sectors, this is referred to as a 'horizontal effect'. When it comes to influence on the policy of provinces and municipalities, the term 'vertical effect' is used. **Performance can be defined in a strict and in a loose sense.** In a strict sense, performance means that the central government itself remains responsible for the policy that has been implemented. There is a top-down process, the policy effectiveness of which can ultimately be determined by effect measurement. This rarely happens in spatial planning; the only exceptions are the large-scale infrastructural works such as the Betuweroute and HSL South, as mentioned before.

In case of **performance in a loose sense**, the question is (only) whether the spatial policy has been described in official documents of the provinces and municipalities in a way that corresponds with the text and the intentions of central government policy. This can be divided into 'conformity', 'use', and 'communication'. 'Conformity' is about literally adopting policy or policy intentions. The result is a paper product (a vision, study, etc.). 'Use' refers to the translation of the policy intention to one's own situation. This could possibly result in subsequent actions or interventions by organizations at lower spatial scales. 'Communication' deals with whether the policy message is transferred to third parties. The result is noticeable through changes in the actual spatial layout.

Performance in the looser sense is most common in Dutch spatial planning. This type of performance can be seen as a process of plan implementation. The aim is to exert influence on various actors in a policy network from (parts of) a plan, for example, a government memorandum. Such a policy is never legally binding. In fact, the policy is sometimes referred to by the term 'indicative policy' and is largely intended as a stimulus. The central issue of performance is the extent to which government policy functions as an external impulse in the municipal context. The main point to note here is that the reality of the municipality is (partially) a different reality than that of the national government. In practice, both parties also have different ways to achieve a strong or weak performance. The national government, for instance, has legal powers to exert direct influence on local spatial developments (e.g., realization of hydrogen infrastructure). Alternatively, municipalities often suffice with stating that national indicative policies are merely taken into consideration ("in all reasonableness") in the implementation of local spatial plans.

Modern approaches conceive **policy implementation** in a way that allows for a certain amount of leeway in interpreting policy objectives. While policy programming provides 'rules of the game', the game (i.e., the implementation) still has to be played (Knoepfel *et al.* 2011). Such an approach can be considered as **policy performance**. Performance is evaluated against "the usefulness of a policy in decision-making process" (Shahab *et al.* 2019, p. 543). A policy implementation performs well "if and only if it plays a tangible role in the choices of the actors to whom it is addressed" (Mastop and Faludi 1997). Such an evaluation helps to understand what happens to policy in the implementation phase; however, it is a less positivistic understanding of policy implementation, acknowledging that the implementation process of policy objectives can also encounter value conflicts inherent in the policy objectives. This applies in particular to complex and multi-faceted policy objectives.

In line with the previous chapters, each essential policy aspect is also assumed to have support in society and thus represents the prevailing values and norms (**'normativity'**) of that society. In other words, it is 'a child of its time'. At the same time, however, policy in its turn also influences the same values and norms (Chapin 1965). In this way, new policy also influences the needs and wishes and possibly the formulation of subsequent policy intentions of municipalities. It can also influence the planning of alternatives and the subsequent choices and actions. The conclusion of this section is that, from a planning perspective, in practice the policy freedom of municipalities is considerable. However, many people, including members of city councils, still have a strong top-down view of planning practice. As a result, the misrepresentation of many seems to determine the practice of policy implementation. In other words, a lack of knowledge of planning limits the available options in many municipalities.

4.3 Discussion: societal developments and uncertain and complex planning challenges

The context of planning is increasingly shaped by **new societal challenges** such as climate change and related adaptation and mitigation strategies of cities (Snel *et al.* 2020), the global COVID-19 pandemic and its socio-spatial consequences, the energy transition and its demands on a (circular) restructuring of real estates (e.g., residential properties that do not use natural gas), growing attention to smart city and the potential of innovations in digital knowledge technologies for the future lay-out and functioning of cities (Jiang *et al.* 2020), changing real estate markets (e.g., regional variation in supply and demand of housing), urban accessibility and transitions to more sustainable forms of mobility (Suprayoga *et al.* 2020b), etc. These new planning challenges increasingly highlight the tensions mentioned before (e.g., flexibility vs. legal certainty) and in that sense also point at shortcomings of the formal planning system to cope with this uncertainty efficiently and effectively, but also in a legitimate and just way (Needham *et al.* 2018).

These new **complex and uncertain planning challenges are reflected in all parts of the planning triangle.** Depending on the planning issue (object) and the way in which those involved look at it (process), emphasis can be placed on the influence of context variables on the object, or the influence of context variables on the process. We have already observed changes in spatial planning practice, which, in terms of the object of planning, are most clearly reflected in growing attention to the materialization of substantive planning problems at the regional scale (Van Straalen and Witte 2018). Next to this, in terms of the process of planning, we have seen an increasing focus on 'governance' as a common response to a changing object matter. The context thus provides the preconditions within which substantive (object) and procedural (process) objectives can be achieved. At the same time, the context is mainly formed by the aspects discussed in the previous two sections: the administrative organization on the one hand and the institutional preconditions (legislation and regulations within the formal planning system) on the other hand. In terms of the administrative and institutional context, formally, the upcoming Environment and Spatial Planning Act is a response to a changing society and the new spatial challenges that come along with that.

Spatial scale and wider societal developments

Spatial scale is an important element in analyzing new planning challenges in the light of societal developments. On the one hand, in the physical domain (i.e., in the 'hardware'), we can see that relational systems of human interactions are growing, and this increases the spatial scale on which these interactions take place. Instead of administrative or territorial boundaries such as municipal borders, now organizational or social boundaries become more important in defining the scope of networks. Increasingly this is taking place at the regional scale (Lester and Reckhow 2013; Evers and Vries 2013; Lambregts *et al.* 2008). On the other hand, in the non-physical or mental domain (i.e., in the 'software'), we can see a growing desire for more locally and contextually bound interactions, for example, remote-working spaces within the own neighbourhood, where people can meet, work, etc., in local libraries, station areas, or similar locales. This process is visible at multiple spatial scales. All of this implies that scale is a relational construct, and that many relational interactions at different spatial scales have implications for how land-use planning is organized.

Looking at society at large, a few societal developments are worth mentioning in the light of the scale issue and increasing uncertainty in the context of planning. A few of these challenges (i.e., globalization and its related economic and demographic changes) have already been happening for a longer time, and their cumulative effects on land-use planning are already quite visible. These issues will first be discussed. Following that, we will briefly discuss two of the more recent societal challenges that were already mentioned at the beginning of this section, namely, climate change and COVID-19, which certainly have relevance for spatial planning, but their implications are still very much in development and are therefore less clear.

Globalization and localization

Globalization of social and economic processes is happening both physically, virtually, and culturally. Citizens, governments, and businesses are less bound to one specific location. As a result of this, the national and international levels are increasingly organized – at least in economic terms – based on the notion of the network society (Castells 2011). This means, among other things, that many enterprises worldwide are less bound by the spatial proximity of their customers. At the same time, as just mentioned, a need for more 'human' interaction is also growing (Kearns and Paddison 2000), and, further, the COVID-19-crisis has triggered some countermovement to globalization. For spatial planning, globalization can have substantial effects not only in terms of demand and type of land-uses, but it also can have severe consequences for land policy (Thiel 2018).

Development of economic sectors

Related to the previous societal development is the **change of economic sectors**, and in particular the increasing attention to commercial services (i.e., third sector) – often at the expense of shrinking agricultural and industrial sectors (i.e., first and second sector). This is reinforcing the 'footloose' or less spatially bound nature of the global economies. Regardless of the tension between the global and the local as mentioned before, we can see that the regional dimension in the distribution of economic activities (e.g., the Randstad) is and will remain of importance (Lambregts *et al.* 2008), and that indicators such as the gross regional product, regional production, or regional employment are not very much influenced by changing organizational structures that arise within the network society.

Demographic developments

Also changes in **demographic developments** and compositions are relevant for planning. In general, demographic growth is slowing down, mostly influenced by shrinking natural population growth (i.e., less reproduction and smaller families). Alongside this development, immigration is becoming a more important factor in the growth and distribution of the population. Together with urbanization, this is leading to selective growth in certain places – mostly in the urbanized areas – whereas other areas are shrinking – mostly the more peripheral areas. Especially in shrinking rural areas, where the percentage of elderly people is rising, demand for facilities is decreasing, unemployment is rising, and young people are leaving – this can have serious implications for future land-use planning (Meijer 2018). This is leading to a different scope and distribution of spatial claims, for instance, in terms of supply and demand – both quantitatively and qualitatively – for housing in different areas. In addition, infrastructure, recreation, nature development, etc., are demanding more space. As mentioned, this is likely coinciding with a growing supply of sites that were formerly used for agricultural or industrial purposes.

Cumulative effects for land-use planning

The developments mentioned here are cumulatively leading to **two important consequences for land-use planning**. First, pressure to free up space for urban functions is increasing, especially in terms of residential development and infrastructure development. At least in the

Netherlands, this is happening simultaneously with shrinking demand for agriculture, which is increasingly characterized by a smaller number of large-scale and specialized agricultural companies. The 'traditional' farms, on the other hand, are increasingly used for recreational and leisurely purposes. The second and related consequence is that these developments in land supply and demand are oftentimes spatially and functionally incompatible. Even though demand for urban housing and infrastructure is increasing, and supply of vacant agricultural sites is also increasing, this is not necessarily happening at similar locations throughout a country or region.

Climate change

As mentioned, planning also has to deal with progressively more implications of climate change for **climate adaptation and mitigation** strategies in cities. Extreme weather events, such as floods, droughts, water scarcity, or heat waves demand new responses and concepts to enable climate scientists and governments to address negative impacts of climate change on people and the environment (Snel *et al.* 2020). Climate change also influences the fundamentals of planning: property rights (Tarlock 2012; Van Straalen *et al.* 2018). Urban areas are likely to be affected, as they are especially vulnerable to the impacts of a warmer climate because of urbanization pressure and aging infrastructures (IPCC 2014). For instance, urban areas worldwide are facing increasing flood risks due to sea-level rise, increasing heavy rainfall, and rising groundwater levels (Snel *et al.* 2020). Urban resilience to extreme weather events integrates social, ecological, and technological systems to provide adequate infrastructures to withstand a warmer climate (Tempels and Hartmann 2014). This has implications for current modes of governance, decision-making processes, and a change of the current social practices of urban planning (Greiving 2002). This makes climate adaptation an important new task of spatial planning.

The COVID-19 pandemic

A more recent example of a societal development that has severe consequences for spatial planning and how to deal with uncertainty and complexity is the global COVID-19 **pandemic**. During the relatively short time span of this pandemic, already a lot of academic reflections have been published, in the realm of spatial planning and governance (e.g., Janssen and Van der Voort 2020) as in other fields. Attention is, for instance, going to the process of planning in terms of best practices and approaches to governing the pandemic (He *et al.* 2021) and the role of big data and artificial intelligence (Bragazzi *et al.* 2020). More attention is also afforded to how the pandemic is affecting other facets of our society and its (spatial) planning, including the economy (Akbulaev *et al.* 2020), aspects of justice (Choi *et al.* 2021), or urban mobility (Park 2020).

Although the pandemic is still ongoing at the time of writing this book, it is also interesting to reflect on the potential (long-term) implications of COVID-19 from a spatial planning perspective. For instance, in terms of participation and the role of the government, this could entail that the pandemic has been a forced window of opportunity for people to engage in online communication; accordingly, this can pave the way for more e-governance approaches in the future. It could also be that people have gained more respect and/or trust in the central government taking the lead, thus they may expect similar guidance for future spatial developments (or, of course, the other way around). In terms of spatial implications, it could be that people are so historically/path-dependently/institutionally wired, that they will lapse back into the 'old normal' as soon as this is possible again and, for instance, the daily commuting patterns will return to the old pre-pandemic levels. However, it is possible that, due to strict lockdowns, people are more oriented towards their own neighbourhood and are therefore more likely to engage in remote working and local participatory planning practices in the future.

From these last examples it is mostly seen that **spatial planning is 'a mirror of society'**, and, in that sense, it remains to be seen how planners will respond to these challenges in the future. One thing that is certain, however, is that the context always is and will remain uncertain. That brings us to the conclusions of this chapter.

4.4 Conclusion: increasing uncertainty

This chapter has examined the administrative and institutional context of planning and the relation of contextual variables with planning.

Within the administrative context, the **allocation of municipal finances is of prime importance** for understanding the administrative context of planning in the Netherlands. The financial flows from the national government to the provinces and municipalities are an important control instrument for the national government. Two main mechanisms are relevant here. First, the subsidiarity principle, which dictates that everything the 'lower' governmental layer can do, it also must do. The second mechanism is the pursuit of egalitarianism, which explains why many facilities in municipalities across the Netherlands look so similar.

One of the practical results of this way of organizing the administrative context is that the 'lower' governmental layers are partly autonomous, which means self-determined. Striving for egalitarianism, however, requires a strong grasp of higher-level authorities. And this again is at odds with the **principle of subsidiarity**. So, it is becoming clear that this is a recurring dilemma that requires striking a balance between the respective interests of different governmental layers. Through financing flows, the national government can regulate to some extent how municipalities should allocate their resources for specific matters. Even though, at first sight, this administrative context seems to restrict what planners can or cannot do at the local level, this changes when the institutional context of planning is considered.

Where the administrative context for municipalities consists of regulations and money flows, the situation in **spatial planning practice is different**. This is reflected in the institutional context of planning. The institutional context is largely shaped by the so-called coordination structure (i.e., the formal planning system), which is anchored in the law. The coordination between the three government layers (national government, province, and municipality) thus appears to be formally regulated. The national government formulates strategic policy for the longer term, the province pursues a tactical policy for the medium term within this framework, and the municipality has an operational policy within the given frameworks.

This **classic coordination structure has long been abandoned in the Netherlands**. After all, formal legislation is only of a procedural nature. The substantive policy of the central government is almost entirely indicative. The consequence of this is that, for the most part, this policy should only be considered 'in all reasonableness' when making decisions at the municipal level. The effect (the 'performance') of formal governmental policy is therefore limited in practice. Even though one can question whether this relative freedom of municipalities is actually embraced by them (mostly not, due to lacking knowledge and/or resources), it does provide a large degree of flexibility for planning. This is useful, since it allows room for open planning processes, informal networks, and extra-legal plans.

Finally, in the light of the planning triangle, it has become clear that context variables are also very much related to substantive (object) or procedural (process) elements of planning. This is mostly visible in how contextual developments in society at large (e.g., climate change, COVID-19, etc.) impact the complexity of land-use planning ('context to object') and how contextual developments in the legal system (e.g., the upcoming implementation of the Environment and Spatial Planning Act) impact the complexity of governance and institutional arrangements ('context to process'). The final chapter of this book will further elaborate on how object, process, and context are internally interrelated – and why this also must be so in order to keep on responding to the ever-changing nature of the spatial reality that planners have to deal with.

5 Discussion
The planning triangle 'revisited'

Spatial planning implements spatial public policy. This implementation, however, does not take place in a vacuum. The planning triangle provides an analytical lens to better understand and conceptualize spatial planning interventions. This final chapter therefore brings together the three dimensions of the planning triangle and explores the ways in which the planning triangle can be an analytical and a conceptual tool for spatial planning practice and research, using the 'Utrecht school' of spatial planning as an example of this.

5.1 Defined or open

The object, process, and context of planning can be either clearly defined or open. The distinction between well-defined and open is discussed in literature with different terminologies and nuances. In relation to planning, Moroni (2010) refers to teleocratic and nomocratic regulatory approaches. Here, the teleocratic approach describes "a directional set of authoritative rules established with the end of achieving a desired overall state of affairs" (Moroni 2010, p. 138) and the nomocratic approach is described as "basic and plain rules that refer to general types of situations or actions, not to specific ones" (p. 146). Needham et al. (2018) distinguish, based on legal traditions, condition-based and performance-based regulations. Condition-based regulations leave less scope for discretion but define precisely what needs to be done and under which conditions; performance-based regulations determine the desired performance of a regulated object – a city or a district – and requires concretization during the implementation (Fonk 2010; Albrecht and Wendler 2009). These distinctions show that there are degrees of how defined or open planning issues can be. This has consequences for the object, process, and context of planning.

DOI: 10.4324/9781003230489-5

5.1.1 Defined and open objects of planning

If the **planning object is well defined and undisputed**, it is very clear and measurable what needs to be realized. The aim to produce a certain amount of new residential units within a certain period (e.g., the 'residential development task' of the Utrecht region to build tens of thousands of dwellings before 2040), for example, is a very clear planning objective regarding the object. Also, the construction of a new highspeed railway connection from urban region A to urban region B (e.g., the HSL South from Amsterdam to Brussels), the development of an intermodal freight corridor between a port and its hinterland (e.g., the Betuweroute), or the realization of a certain amount of flood retention volumes (e.g., the water retention objectives that are formulated in the masterplan of the Feyenoord City megaproject in Rotterdam) are examples of clearly defined planning objectives regarding the planning objects. The plan implementation can then be measured against its effectiveness in achieving such goals, thus the conformance of planning objects with planning objectives can be assessed clearly. The implication for planning is that it needs to be more rigid and executive while providing less scope for balancing and discretion in interpreting policy objectives.

If the **planning object is less defined and more open** – such as the vision for sustainable, resilient, or smart cities – the implementation of such planning requires a different approach and more flexibility regarding the planning object. For instance, the National Environmental Vision (*NOVI*) draws attention to the sizeable spatial claims that are needed for 'building dwellings, generating sustainable energy, dealing with climate change and the transition towards a circular economy'. Open definitions of the planning objects require more balancing – such as balancing economic, environmental, and social issues of sustainability. Instead of conformance, performance of policy implementation is more relevant. The openness regarding the planning object also implies a greater need for interpretation of policy objectives by planners and more room for discretion.

Vague or open definitions of the planning object can result from multiple interpretations from various stakeholders' perspectives regarding the nature of the problem. Also, uncertainty regarding the context of planning increases the openness of planning objects. **Uncertainty** describes the difficulty of predicting the outcomes of actions, **normativity** describes a situation in which not a single truth exists but rather plural perceptions (Hendriks 1999) resulting from different interpretations of the world by different stakeholders (Baum 1977, p. 414).

This is described by Forester, who concludes that planning is "situated 'in between' conflicting or at least disputing parties" (Forester 2004, p. 246). So, normativity in the relation between planning objects and processes and uncertainty with regard to the relation between object and context increases openness and obstructs defined planning objects (Figure 5.1).

5.1.2 *Defined and open processes of planning*

Also **planning processes can be either well defined or open.** This distinction can be linked to different approaches to legitimation of planning outcomes. Legitimation for planning can be earned via different forms of legitimacy: "if the state body is recognised by the public as acting on their behalf (input); if the body follows the procedures prescribed for protecting citizens' rights (throughput); and if the body produces results which are generally recognised as good (output)" (Needham *et al.* 2018, p. 138). These forms of legitimacy relate to defined (input legitimacy) and open (output legitimacy) planning processes, with throughput legitimacy being an intermediate. Defined planning processes foresee specific procedures and instruments. Examples for defined planning processes are classical Euclidian zoning (Elliott 2008) or functional land-use planning that separates land-uses. Such planning processes clearly define the administrative and procedural aspects of planning.

In contrast, **participatory, collaborative, or inclusive planning processes** are often more open than top-down modes of governance. Consequently, open planning processes need to balance different intervention strategies – sticks, carrots, or sermons; different strategies of plan implementation, etc., while in some sectoral planning regimes in particular planning processes are often more defined and straightforward (such as water management; Hartmann and Spit 2014).

In recent decades, a **trend towards more open planning processes** due to **increasing pluralism** (i.e., normativity) has developed in society but also a trend towards integrated planning approaches. In particular, the post-positivist notion in planning theory (Allmendinger 2002) supports that pluralistic and more normative relations between the planning object and planning processes can be described in terms of **increasing normativity**. At the same time, planning processes need to increasingly integrate more issues – the recent Dutch Environmental and Spatial Planning Act is a prime example of this trend. The relation between planning processes and planning context can therefore be described in terms of **complexity** (Figure 5.1).

5.1.3 Defined and open contexts of planning

Context can be well defined or open as well. The reconstruction after World War II, for example, provided a clear definition of the context, in which the socio-economic circumstances as well as environmental issues clearly appeared. Rittel and Webber denoted planning problems of that time as 'tame' problems, which were relatively "definable, understandable and consensual" (Rittel and Webber 1973, p. 156). Since that time, rationalism (Baum 1977) and positivism (Allmendinger 2002) have been increasingly rejected as prevalent planning paradigms. In contrast, planning problems are now more commonly acknowledged as being 'wicked problems', which means they are more complex and less predictable problems. The recent changes in the context of spatial planning increase the wickedness and uncertainty: societal developments such as dealing with pandemics, climate change, mobility and energy transitions, populistic political contexts, etc., contribute to more dynamic and open planning contexts.

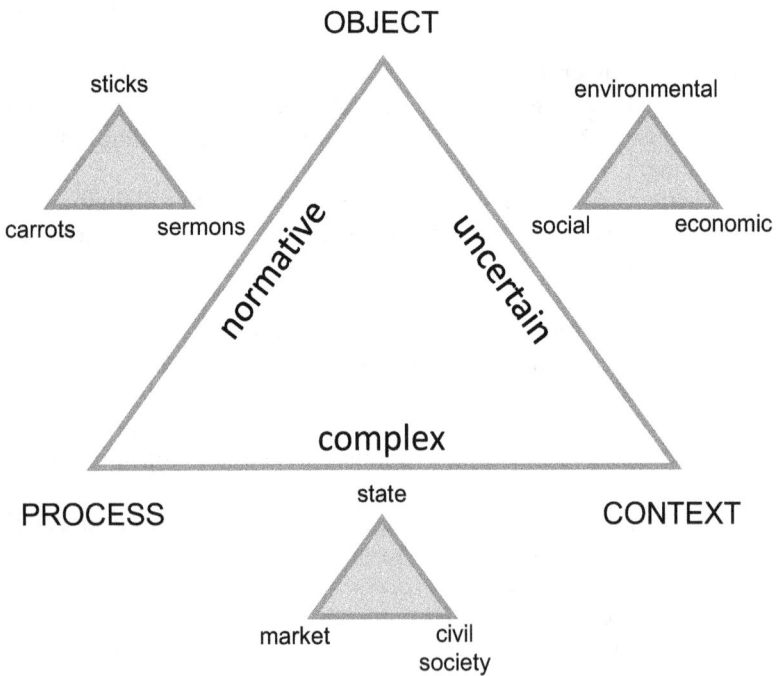

Figure 5.1 Balancing the planning triangle: normativity, complexity, and uncertainty

In relation to planning processes, planning contexts that are less defined or tame but more open and wicked instead **increase complexity**. In complex planning situations the identification of planning problems goes beyond rationalist reasoning (Roo and Silva 2010; Gunder and Hillier 2010). "Complexity implies that establishing a line of argument along objectively-rational axioms based on rationalistic methods and bureaucratic rules is not easy" (Hartmann 2012, p. 244). Complexity thus has consequences for the governance of planning issues; therefore, complexity affects the interrelations of state, market, and civil society.

5.1.4 Dynamics of object, process, and context

So, analytically and practically, the object, process, and context of planning – being defined or open – are very much related to each other. The relation between the three dimensions of the planning triangle can be further described and understood through reflecting on the notions of **normativity, complexity, and uncertainty** (Figure 5.1). While there is a lure for planners to address planning issues as 'defined' in terms of object, process, and context, addressing the 'openness' of the three corners of planning is much more challenging. In looking at the current state of spatial planning in the Netherlands, it can be argued that we are moving towards ever more open planning situations, characterized by plurality, wicked problems, and non-linear 'change events' (Teisman *et al.* 2009). Figure 5.1 presents a scheme that can be useful in analytically deducting what is happening in the balancing act between normativity, uncertainty, and complexity. In the relation between object and process, different intervention approaches – sticks, carrots, sermons – can help to find the most suitable strategy in a particular (open or closed) planning situation. In the relation between process and context, the relation of state, market, and civil society is useful to explore options to deal with the complexity. The triangle of sustainability – environmental, social, and economic aspects – can help planners to balance the issues within the relation between object and context. Figure 5.1 does not provide a recipe, but it can be a way to use the planning triangle conceptually, so that planning can better address the openness of object, process, and context.

In the next section, we will explore the history and evolution of planning education and research at Utrecht University, to showcase how the planning triangle has both been instrumental in the development of the 'Utrecht school' of planning, but also how it can still function as an analytical lens to reflect in hindsight on how certain aspects of spatial planning have gained either more or less prominence in spatial planning discussions over time.

5.2 The 'Utrecht school': evolution of planning education and research

As was already mentioned in the Foreword to this book, planning education and research at Utrecht University take on a special and significant position (Spit and Zoete 2009). In this, the planning triangle has been an important analytical lens that is intrinsically linked to the 'Utrecht' approach to understanding spatial planning in the Netherlands, as is outlined in this book. Therefore, planning education and research in the light of the planning triangle deserve specific attention here, to both explain the significance of the planning triangle but also its analytical use in understanding how the Utrecht tradition developed over time. This approach is founded on the academic work of professor Ton Kreukels.

In one of his key publications, Kreukels considers planning as 'a mirror of societal developments' on the basis of a study trip through the United States (Kreukels 1985). We have also referred to this function of spatial planning throughout this book. To this day, Kreukels is seen as one of the first to question the then structuralist 'inside-out' planning approach (Boelens 2011). In 'inside-out' planning, a limited group of 'insiders' (i.e., planners and administrators) designed spatial plans for the wider benefit of society (i.e., the outsiders or recipients or beneficiaries of planning efforts). In contrast, Kreukels' approach had affinity with the urban regime theories at that time (Fainstein 1986; Logan and Molotch 1987) and advocated a form of planning that involved various stakeholders in spatial planning (Boelens 2011).

Now, more than 30 years after this initial publication, it is still occasionally referred to in Dutch spatial planning debates. Spatial planning, so Kreukels argued, is not only mundane and ubiquitous but even desirable. After all, planning is anchored in a societal background as well as in an institutional environment. Planning can therefore only be studied adequately if it is positioned against this same societal and institutional background. In the 1990s, spatial planning research at Utrecht University mainly developed along this line, meaning along the lines of an institutional approach towards spatial planning. We will review this development along the different analytical dimensions of the planning triangle: object-, process-, and context-orientation.

Object-orientation: mainport development

In terms of the object of planning, mainport development was given a prominent place in the research programme in the course of the 1990s. In a more general sense, the dominance of the object of planning in Utrecht University's urban planning research is reflected in the close collaborations of Professor Kreukels and Professor Spit with the Human Geography Department that originated in the 1990s (Dieleman *et al.* 1999) and continued until very recently (e.g., Yang *et al.* 2019). More specifically, Kreukels' research at that time focused on the development of seaports (Kreukels and Wever 1998) while Spit researched the development of railway station locations (Spit and Bertolini 1998). Both specializations have a continuing legacy in more recent academic work on maritime ports (Witte *et al.* 2018), inland ports (Witte *et al.* 2019), and railway station areas (De Wijs *et al.* 2016). Following the *Cities on Rails* book by Spit and Bertolini (1998), the node-place model was also developed by Professor Bertolini (Bertolini 1999), which was later often used by other researchers (e.g., Peek *et al.* 2006; Vale 2015). The special approach of research into mainport development, with a focus on the relationship between mainports and their surroundings, is appreciated in the scientific discussion, because the traditional research from this time focused mostly on a sectoral analysis of transport (nodes) (Docherty 2000). This special combination of linking research themes with planning and geographical perspectives can also be found later in doctoral research projects by Utrecht spatial planning scholars (Witte 2014; Yang 2018; Delphine 2019; Suprayoga 2020). Also, the combination of geographical and planning perspectives is visible in the special appointment of Edwin Buitelaar as Professor for land and real estate development.

Process-orientation: institutional and actor-relational approaches

In terms of the process of planning, in the beginning of the 2000s, a substantive change took place when Kreukels focused more on the actor-oriented approach, while Spit returned more theoretically to the institutional approach as the basis for planning research (Needham *et al.* 2000). The actor-oriented approach can be seen as an attempt by Kreukels to develop a new theoretical perspective on urban planning that mediated between a behavioural science approach and an approach more focused on public administration. This can be observed in the book *Planning without Government* (Boelens *et al.* 2006, Dutch title translated by authors). This actor-oriented approach is linked to the institutional approach, as shown in the book *Metropolitan Governance and Spatial Planning: Comparative Case Studies of European City-regions* by Salet *et al.* (2003) on strategic planning.

With the appointment of Boelens as professor in 2004, the actor-oriented approach in a theoretical sense received an important impulse. This is elaborated upon in the actor-relational planning approach (Boelens 2010), which is also often discussed in the international literature under the wider umbrella of actor-network theory (ANT) (e.g., Rydin 2010). According to this approach, the contrast between modern and post-modern planning can be better understood – and planning can be better guided – by a greater emphasis on the actor-orientation as a substitute for government centrism. Boelens mainly points out the disadvantages of this traditional government-oriented way of practising planning with what he refers to as failing planning projects or concepts such as the Betuweline or the Green Heart in the Randstad (Boelens 2011). This actor-oriented approach not only tries to minimize uncertainties, fragmentation, or pluralism as in the traditional approach, but also looks for possibilities outside of the traditional approach (Boelens 2011). Here, an important characteristic of the theoretical perspective of the planning research at Utrecht University becomes visible again: the continuous reflection on the complex interaction between the public and private spheres. This is also prominently visible in the current research programme 'Governance of Urban Transitions' that is led by the current Professors Monstadt and Frantzeskaki.

Context-orientation: sustainable urban futures and digitalization of cities

In terms of the context of planning, from 2010 onwards, another paradigm shift has taken place in Utrecht University's planning research: an orientation towards the sustainable design of the living environment and futures of cities is becoming increasingly central. The programmatic collaboration started at that time with the current Copernicus Institute of Sustainable Development at Utrecht University. This opened up new perspectives on theory development, which are particularly focused on research into different (sustainable) modes of governance (Driessen and Spit 2010; Hartmann and Driessen 2017) and related societal challenges such as addressing climate change (Snel 2021). Next to the increasing focus on sustainable urban futures as an important linking pin to societal developments at large, another more recent context-orientation of the Utrecht planning research is concerned with the digitalization of cities and the potential role of technology in supporting spatial planning. This was started with the appointment of Geertman as professor in 2016. Recent research has focused particularly on the role and potential of smart urban governance in transforming cities (Jiang 2021).

To conclude, in our opinion, the way in which theoretical insights can be applied to problems in spatial planning practices remains a key characteristic of spatial planning research and teaching at Utrecht University. In today's societal context, with a strong emphasis on dealing with complex urban transitions, it is less relevant whether the object of planning includes economic themes or sustainability themes. Contemporary research is looking for 'governance solutions' for such transitions in the process of planning that provide an answer to increasing normativity, complexity, and uncertainty within planning issues in different contexts.

5.3 Epilogue by the authors

This book opened with a reference to the AESOP and their rationale of what planning education shall achieve: "Planning education involves the scientific study of and training in creative conceptual and practical thinking on the relation between society and environment at various territorial levels and in the search, development and advancement of opportunities for purposeful intervention in that relation to ensure sustainable development" (AESOP Core requirements for a high-quality European Planning Education).

In this spirit, this book set out to provide an analytical and conceptual framework to approach practical spatial planning problems. The planning triangle is no more but also no less than 'just' a framework. Many details of spatial planning as an academic discipline, the way it is exercised, and of the Dutch legal system for spatial planning are purposefully only touched upon at the surface level or have even been left out altogether. For example, the topic and details of land policy in the Netherlands (e.g., Van Oosten *et al.* 2018), which is highly relevant for the Dutch context, have been left out. The idea behind this is that we want to mainly provide a first and introductory orientation on the broad discipline of spatial planning – with reference to the Netherlands – and we want to motivate the readers of this book to seek further reading on specific topics on their own. For land policy and property rights, consider for instance Barrie Needham's work on planning law, land economics or Dutch land-use planning (Needham *et al.*

2018; Needham 2014). We conceive a further study highly relevant to dive deeper into the specifics of the objects, processes, and contexts of planning. This entails, amongst others, a further understanding of the plurality of planning theories (note that in 2021 a new thematic group of AESOP on planning theories has been established), a diversity of planning methods, and raising awareness for the societal and institutional dynamics in the planning context.

By focusing on the planning triangle of object, process, and context, this book is also an obeisance to the "era Spit" in the Dutch, and especially Utrecht University's, approach to spatial planning. Tejo Spit was one of the core full professors who established the teaching and research at Utrecht's planning school along the dimensions of object, process, and context. This book tries to reflect upon and further develop the pedigree of this approach. At the same time, this book can also be considered a goodbye to and by Thomas Hartmann, who spent 11 years teaching and researching Dutch spatial planning. Thomas Hartmann now left the Netherlands to go to Germany and took up the position of Chair of the Land Policy and Land Management department as full professor at TU Dortmund. Patrick Witte continues the Utrecht planning tradition in both the bachelor's programme of Human Geography and Planning, and in the master's programme of Spatial Planning at Utrecht University.

Ultimately, in the enthusiastic spirit of Paul Zoete who wrote the Foreword, this book has been created to serve future generations of Dutch planning students as an introduction and orientation to the exciting field of spatial planning. In his lectures, Paul Zoete used to define spatial planning as the 'strategic organisation of hopes and expectations'. Spatial planning was, is, and will be a discipline and profession for optimists. With this book, we hope to contribute to that bright future perspective.

References

AESOP criteria: www.aesop-planning.eu/enGB/core-curriculum

Akbulaev, N., Mammadov, I., and Aliyev, V., 2020. Economic impact of COVID-19. *SSRN Electronic Journal*, 164 (5), 113–126.

Albers, G., 1969. Über das Wesen der räumlichen Planung. Versuch einer Standortbestimmung. *Stadtbauwelt* (21), 10–14.

Albrecht, J., Wendler, W., 2009. Koordinierte Anwendung von Wasserrahmenrichtlinie und Hochwasserrisikomanagementrichtlinie im Kontext des Planungsprozesses. *Natur und Recht*, 31, 608–618.

Albrechts, L., 2004. Strategic (spatial) planning re-examined. *Environment and Planning B: Planning and Design*, 31 (5), 743–758.

Alexander, E.R., 2000. Rationality revisited: Planning paradigms in a post-postmodernist perspective. *Journal of Planning Education and Research*, 19 (3), 242–256.

Alexander, E.R., 2002. The public interest in planning. From legitimation to substantive plan evaluation. *Planning Theory*, 1 (3), 226–249.

Allmendinger, P., 2002. Towards a post-positivist typology of planning theory. *Planning Theory*, 1 (1), 77–99.

Allmendinger, P., and Haughton, G., 2010. Spatial planning, devolution, and new planning spaces. *Environment and Planning C: Government and Policy*, 28, 803–818.

Allmendinger, P., and Tewdwr-Jones, M., 2002. *Planning futures. New directions for planning theory*. London, New York, NY: Routledge.

Ansell, C., and Torfing, J., eds., 2016. *Handbook on theories of governance*. Northampton, MA: Edward Elgar Publishing.

Arnstein, S.R., 1969. A ladder of citizen participation. *AIP Journal*, 35 (4), 216–224.

Arthur, W.B., 1989. Competing technologies increasing returns and lock-in by historical events. *The Economic Journal* (99), 116–131.

Baum, H.S., 1977. Toward a post-industrial planning theory. *Policy Sciences*, 8 (4), 401–421.

Bertolini, L., 1999. Spatial development patterns and public transport: The application of an analytical model in the Netherlands. *Planning Practice and Research*, 14 (2), 199–210.

Bertolini, L., Curtis, C., and Renne, J., 2012. Station area projects in Europe and beyond: Towards transit oriented development? *Built Environment*, 38 (1), 31–50.

Boelens, L., 2009. *The urban connection. An actor-relational approach to urban planning*. Rotterdam: 010 Publishers.

Boelens, L., 2010. Theorizing practice and practising theory: Outlines for an actor-relational-approach in planning. *Planning Theory*, 9 (1), 28–62.

Boelens, L., 2011. Going beyond planners' dependencies: An actor-relational approach to Mainport Rotterdam. *Town Planning Review*, 82 (5), 547–572.

Boelens, L., Spit, T., and Kreukels, T., 2006. *Planning zonder overheid, een toekomst voor planning*. Rotterdam: 010 Publishers.

Boschma, R., Coenen, L., Frenken, K., and Truffer, B., 2017. Towards a theory of regional diversification: combining insights from Evolutionary Economic Geography and Transition Studies. *Regional Studies*, 51 (1), 31–45.

Bragazzi, N.L., *et al.*, 2020. How Big Data and Artificial Intelligence can help better manage the COVID-19 pandemic. *International Journal of Environmental Research and Public Health*, 17 (9).

Bromley, D.W., 1991. *Environment and economy. Property rights and public policy*. Cambridge, MA: B. Blackwell.

Bromley, D.W., 2000. Regulatory takings and land use conflicts. In: M.D. Kaplowitz, ed. *Property rights, economics, and the environment*. Stamford, CT: JAI Press, 23–33.

Brownill, S., and Carpenter, J., 2007. Participation and planning. Dichotomies, rationalities and strategies for power. *TPR*, 78 (4), 401–428.

Bruijn, J.A., de Jong, P., Korsten, A.F.A., and van Zanten, W.P.C., 1996. *Grote projecten; besluitvorming and management*. Alphen a/d Rijn: Samsom H.D. Tjeenk Willink.

Bruinsma, F.R., Rienstra, S.A., and Rietveld, P., 1997. Economic impacts of the construction of a transport corridor: A multi-level and multiapproach case study for the construction of the A1 highway in the Netherlands. *Regional Studies*, 31 (4), 391–402.

Bryson, J.M., 2004. What to do when Stakeholders matter. *Public Management Review*, 6 (1), 21–53.

Buitelaar, E., 2010. Cracks in the myth. Challenges to land policy in the Netherlands. *Tijdschrift voor Economische en Sociale Geografie*, 101 (3), 349–356.

Buitelaar, E., 2012. The fraught relationship between planning and regulation. Land use plans and the conflicts in dealing with uncertainty. In: T. Hartmann and B. Needham, eds. *Planning by law and property rights reconsidered*. Farnham: Ashgate, 207–218.

Buitelaar, E., and Witte, P.A., 2011. *Financiering van gebiedsontwikkeling. Een empirische analyse van grondexploitaties*. Den Haag: Planbureau voor de Leefomgeving.

Campbell, S.D., 2016. The planner's triangle revisited: Sustainability and the evolution of a planning ideal that can't stand still. *Journal of the American Planning Association*, 82 (4), 388–397.

Castells, M., 2011. *The rise of the network society* (Vol. 12). West Sussex: John Wiley & Sons.

Cervero, R., 2004. Transit-oriented development in the United States. Experiences, challenges, and prospects. *Transportation Research Board* (102).

Chapin, F.S., 1965. *Urban land use planning*. London, Chicago: University of Illinois Press.

Choi, J., Lee, S., and Jamal, T., 2021. Smart Korea: Governance for smart justice during a global pandemic. *Journal of Sustainable Tourism*, 29 (2–3), 541–550.

Coase, R., 1960. The problem of social cost. *Journal of Law and Economics* (3), 1–44.

Couclelis, H., 2005. "Where has the future gone?" Rethinking the role of integrated land-use models in spatial planning. *Environment and Planning A*, 37 (8), 1353–1371.

Davy, B., 1996. Baulandsicherung: Ursache oder Lösung eines raumordnungspolitischen Paradoxons? *Zeitschrift für Verwaltung*, 21 (2), 193–208.

Davy, B., 1997. *Essential injustice. When legal institutions cannot resolve environmental and land use disputes*. Wien, New York, NY: Springer.

Davy, B., 2005. Bodenpolitik. In: E.-H. Ritter, ed. *Handwörterbuch der Raumordnung*. Hannover: ARL, 117–130.

Davy, B., 2006. *Innovationspotentiale für Flächenentwicklung in schrumpfenden Städten. Flächenmanagement am Beispiel Magdeburgs* [online]. Available from: www.iba-stadtumbau.de/index.php?Innovationspotentiale-fur-Flachenentwicklung-in-schrumpfenden-Stadten-1 [Accessed 21 April 2009].

Davy, B., 2012. *Land policy. A German perspective on planning and property*. Farnham, Surrey: Ashgate.

Debrunner, G., and Hartmann, T., 2020. Strategic use of land policy instruments for affordable housing – Coping with social challenges under scarce land conditions in Swiss cities. *Land Use Policy*, 99, 104993.

De Haes, U., 1995. Discussion and conclusion. In: J.F.T. Schoute, ed. *Scenario studies for the rural environment. Selected and edited proceedings of the Symposium "Scenario Studies for the Rural Environment," Wageningen, the Netherlands, 12–15 September 1994*. Dordrecht: Boston; Kluwer Academic Publishers, 567–569.

Dekker, G., De Klerk, L., Witsen, P.P., and van der Cammen, H., 2012. *The selfmade land: Culture and evolution of urban and regional planning in the Netherlands*. Spectrum.

De Klerk, L., and Van der Wouden, R., 2021. *Ruimtelijke ordening. Geschiedenis van de stedelijke en regionale planning in Nederland, 1200-nu*. Rotterdam: Nai010.

Delphine, D., 2019. *Perceiving the GIANT. Bringing back people into megaprojects: The case of Indonesian development practice*. Utrecht: Utrecht University.

Dembski, S., 2020. 'Organic' approaches to planning as densification strategy? The challenge of legal contextualisation in Buiksloterham, Amsterdam. *Town Planning Review*, 91 (3), 283–303.

Dembski, S., and Salet, W., 2010. The transformative potential of institutions: How symbolic markers can institute new social meaning in changing cities. *Environment and Planning A*, 42 (3), 611–625.

de Ridder, J., and Koeman, N.S.J., 1999. *Naar een hernieuwd ruimtelijk planningstelsel? Publicatie van de Vereniging voor Bouwrecht nr. 27*. Deventer: Kluwer.

de Ridder, J., and Schut, D., 1995. *De WRO in de steigers*. Deventer: Kluwer.

Derksen, W., 1994. Bestemmingsplannen en gemeenten handhaven. In: *Bestuurswetenschappen 1994/1*, 1–5.

De Wijs, L., Witte, P., and Geertman, S., 2016. How smart is smart? Theoretical and empirical considerations on implementing smart city objectives – a case study of Dutch railway station areas. *Innovation: The European Journal of Social Science Research*, 29 (4), 424–441.

Dey Biswas, S., 2020. *Land acquisition and compensation in India. Mysteries of valuation*. 1st ed. Cham: Springer International Publishing; Imprint: Palgrave Macmillan.

Dieleman, F.M., Dijst, M.J., and Spit, T., 1999. Planning the compact city: The Randstad Holland experience. *European Planning Studies*, 7 (5), 605–621.

Dieleman, F.M., and Wegener, M., 2004. Compact city and urban sprawl. *Built Environment*, 30 (4), 308–323.

Diller, C., and Oberding, S., 2017. Der "Strategic Choice Approach": ein in Deutschland unterschätzter Methodenbaukasten für die Raumplanung. *disP – The Planning Review*, 53 (2), 94–108.

Docherty, I., 2000. Book reviews: Cities on rails: The redevelopment of railway station areas. *Urban Studies*, 37 (8), 1464–1466.

Donders, M., Hartmann, T., and Kokx, A., 2014. E-Participation in urban planning: Getting and keeping citizens involved. *International Journal of E-Planning Research*, 3 (2), 54–69.

Dore, D., 2001. Transforming traditional institutions for sustainable natural resource management: History, narratives and evidence from Zimbabwe's communal areas. *African Studies Quarterly*, 5 (3), 1–18.

Douglas, M., 1986. *How institutions think*. 1st ed. Syracuse, NY: Syracuse University Press.

Dreijerink, L., Kruize, H., and van Kamp, I., 2008. *Burgerparticipatie in beleidsvorming. Resultaten van een verkennende literatuurreview*: Rijksinstituut voor Volksgezondheid en Milieu (RIVM).

Driessen, P.P.J., and Spit, T., 2010. De bekostiging van klimaatadaptatie. Argumenten voor een legitieme balans van baten en lasten. *Beleid en Maatschappij* (37), 73–85.

Driessen, P.P.J., et al., 2012. Conceptual framework for the study of shifts in modes of environmental governance – Experiences from the Netherlands. *Environmental Policy and Governance*, 22 (3), 143–160.

Edelenbos, J., 2000. *Proces in vorm. Procesbegeleiding van interactieve beleidsvorming over lokale ruimtelijke projecten.* Utrecht: LEMMA.

Ellickson, R., 1993. Property in Land. *Yale Law Review* (102), 1315–1400.

Elliott, D.L., 2008. *A better way to zone. Ten principles to create more liveable cities.* Washington, DC: Island Press.

Ellis, E., ed., 1999. The principle of proportionality in the laws of Europe. Oxford, Portland, OR: Hart.

European Council of Town Planners (ECTP), 2002. *New Athens charter.* London: ECTP.

Evers, D., and Vries, J. de, 2013. Explaining governance in five mega-city regions: Rethinking the role of hierarchy and government. *European Planning Studies*, 21 (4), 536–555.

Fagence, M., 1977. *Citizen participation in planning.* 1st ed. Oxford, New York, NY: Pergamon Press.

Fainstein, S.S., 1986. *Restructuring the city. The political economy of urban redevelopment.* New York, NY: Longman.

Fainstein, S.S., 2005. Planning theory and the city. *Journal of Planning Education and Research*, 25 (2), 121–130.

Faludi, A., 1994. *Rule and order Dutch planning doctrine in the twentieth century.* [S.l.]: Springer.

Fonk, C.F., 2010. Die konditionale Rechtssetzung in der Tradition Otto Mayers: ein antiquiertes Normstruktur- und Gesetzgebungsmodell? *Deutsches Verwaltungsblatt*, 10, 626–633.

Forester, J., 2004. Reflections on trying to teach planning theory. *Planning Theory and Practice*, 5 (2), 242–251.

Frantzeskaki, N., and De Haan, H., 2009. Transitions: Two steps from theory to policy. *Futures*, 41 (9), 593–606.

Friend, J., and Jessop, N., 2013. *Local government and strategic choice (Routledge revivals): An operational research approach to the processes of public planning.* Oxfordshire: Routledge.

Fujita, M., and Thisse, J.F., 2002. Agglomeration and market interaction. Available from SSRN 315966.

Geertman, S., 2006. Potentials for planning support: A planning-conceptual approach. *Environment and Planning B: Planning and Design*, 33 (6), 863–880.

Gerber, J.-D., et al., 2009. Institutional resource regimes. Towards sustainability through the combination of property-rights theory and policy analysis. *Ecological Economics*, 68 (3), 798–809.

Gerber, J.-D., Hartmann, T., and Hengstermann, A., eds., 2018. *Instruments of land policy. Dealing with scarcity of land.* Oxon: Routledge.

Gerber, J.-D., Nahrath, S., and Hartmann, T., 2017. The strategic use of time-limited property rights in land-use planning. Evidence from Switzerland. *Environment and Planning A*, 94 (4).

Glaeser, E.L., Gyourko, J., and Saiz, A., 2008. Housing supply and housing bubbles. *Journal of Urban Economics*, 64 (2), 198–217.

Goedhart, C., 1982. Een theoretisch kader voor inkomstenverwerving door lagere overheden. In: *Raad voor de Gemeente Financiën, Macht en middelen in de verhouding rijk-lagere overheden.* Den Haag: VNG.

Götze, V., 2021. *Local governments between growth incentives and landthrift ambitions. The influence of the fiscal system on municipal land use policies* [online]. Wageningen University. Available from: https://edepot.wur.nl/532211 [Accessed 22 May 2021].

Graham, S., and Marvin, S., 2002. *Splintering urbanism: Networked infrastructures, technological mobilities and the urban condition.* Oxfordshire: Routledge.

Greiving, S., 2002. *Räumliche Planung und Risiko.* München: Gerling-Akademie Verlag.

Gualini, E., 2010. Governance, space and politics: Exploring the governmentality of planning. In: J. Hillier and P. Healey, eds. *The Ashgate research companion to planning theory. Conceptual challenges for spatial planning.* Farnham, Surrey: Ashgate, 57–85.

Gunder, M., and Hillier, J., 2010. *Planning in ten words or less. A Lacanian entanglement with spatial planning.* Farnham, Surrey: Ashgate.

Gunder, M., Madanipour, A., and Watson, V., eds., 2018. *The Routledge handbook of planning theory.* New York, NY: Routledge.

Gupta, J., Pfeffer, K., Verrest, H., and Ros-Tonen, M., 2015. An inclusive development perspective on the geographies of urban governance. In J. Gupta, K. Pfeffer, H. Verrest, and M. Ros-Tonen, eds. *Geographies of urban governance.* Cham (Switzerland): Springer, 217–228.

Guy, S., and Henneberry, J., 2002. Approaching development. *Development and Developers: Perspectives on Property,* 1–18.

Hajer, M., 2003. Policy without polity? Policy analysis and the institutional void. *Policy Sciences,* 36 (2), 175–195.

Hajer, M.A., and Pelzer, P., 2018. 2050 – An energetic odyssey: Understanding 'Techniques of Futuring' in the transition towards renewable energy. *Energy Research & Social Science,* 44, 222–231.

Hajer, M.A., et al., eds., 2010. *Sterke verhalen. Hoe Nederland de planologie opnieuw uitvindt.* Rotterdam: 010 Publishers.

Hansen, A.H., 1968. *Business cycles and national income.* London: Allen and Unwin.

Hanson, S., and Giuliano, G., eds., 2004. *The geography of urban transportation.* Guilford Press.

Hardin, G., 1968. The tragedy of the commons. *Science,* 162 (3859), 1243–1248.

Hartmann, T., 2012. Wicked problems and clumsy solutions: Planning as expectation management. *Planning Theory,* 11 (3), 242–256.

Hartmann, T., and Driessen, P., 2017. The flood risk management plan: towards spatial water governance. *Journal of Flood Risk Management,* 10 (2), 145–154.

Hartmann, T., and Geertman, S., 2016. Planning theory. In: J. Torfing and C. Ansell, eds. *Handbook on theories of governance.* S.l.: Edward Elgar Publishing.

Hartmann, T., and Gerber, J.-D., 2018. Land, scarcity, and property rights. In: J.-D. Gerber, T. Hartmann, and A. Hengstermann, eds. *Instruments of land policy. Dealing with scarcity of land*. Oxon: Routledge, 3–7.

Hartmann, T., and Hengstermann, A., 2014. Territorial cohesion through spatial policies – An analysis with Cultural Theory and clumsy solutions. *Central European Journal of Public Policy*, 8 (1), 30–49.

Hartmann, T., and Needham, B., eds., 2012. *Planning by law and property rights reconsidered*. Farnham: Ashgate.

Hartmann, T., and Spit, T., 2014. Frontiers of land and water governance in urban regions. *Water International*, 39 (6), 791–797.

Hartmann, T., and Spit, T., 2015a. Dilemmas of involvement in land management – Comparing an active (Dutch) and a passive (German) approach. *Land Use Policy*, 42, 729–737.

Hartmann, T., and Spit, T., 2015b. Towards an integrated water management – Comparing German and Dutch water law from a spatial planning perspective. *International Journal of Water Governance*, 3 (2), 59–78.

Hartmann, T., and Spit, T., 2015c. Theorie toepasbaar op praktijk: planologie in Utrecht. *Rooilijn*, 48 (1), 32–37.

Hartmann, T., and Spit, T., 2016. Legitimizing differentiated flood protection levels – Consequences of the European flood risk management plan. *Environmental Science & Policy*, 55, 361–367.

Hartmann, T., Van Straalen, F., and Spit, T., 2018. Expectation management at the local scale: Legal failure of public participation for large urban planning projects. *TeMA – Journal of Land Use, Mobility and Environment*, 11 (1), 133–145.

He, Q., et al., 2021. Practice in information technology support for Fangcang Shelter Hospital during COVID-19 epidemic in Wuhan, China. *Journal of Medical Systems*, 45 (4), 42.

Healey, P., 1996. The communicative turn in planning theory and its implications for spatial strategy formation. *Environment and Planning B: Planning and Design*, 23, 217–234.

Healey, P., 1997. *Collaborative planning. Shaping places in fragmented societies*. Vancouver: UBC Press.

Healey, P., 2003. Collaborative planning in perspective. *Planning Theory*, 2 (2), 101–123.

Healey, P., 2006. Transforming governance: Challenges of institutional adaptation and a new politics of space. *European Planning Studies*, 14 (3), 299–320.

Hendriks, F., 1999. The post-industrialising city: political perspectives and cultural biases. *GeoJournal* (47), 425–432.

Hengstermann, A., and Hartmann, T., 2021. Kohärente Planungsdidaktik – Eine Würdigung des Projektstudiums. *RaumPlanung*, 210 (1), 21–25.

Hermans, L.M., and Thissen, W.A., 2009. Actor analysis methods and their use for public policy analysts. *European Journal of Operational Research*, 196 (2), 808–818.

Hersperger, A.M., Grădinaru, S., Oliveira, E., Pagliarin, S., and Palka, G., 2019. Understanding strategic spatial planning to effectively guide development of urban regions. *Cities*, 94, 96–105.

Hess, C., and Ostrom, E., 2007. Introduction: An overview of the knowledge commons. In: E. Ostrom, ed. *Understanding knowledge as a commons. From theory to practice*. Cambridge, MA: MIT Press, 3–26.

Hillier, J., 2010. Introduction. Planning at yet another crossroads? In: J. Hillier and P. Healey, eds. *The Ashgate research companion to planning theory. Conceptual challenges for spatial planning*. Farnham, Surrey: Ashgate, 1–34.

Hooghe, L., Marks, G., and Marks, G.W., 2001. *Multi-level governance and European integration*. Rowman & Littlefield.

Howard, E., Howard, E.J., and Ebenezer, H., 1965. *Garden cities of tomorrow* (Vol. 23). Cambridge (MA): Mit Press.

Huxley, M., 2000. The limits to communicative planning. *Journal of Planning Education and Research* (19), 369–377.

Hyatt, D.E., Lenz, R., and Pykh, I.A., 1999. *Environmental indices systems analysis approach*. Oxford: EOLSS.

Innes, J.E., and Booher, D.E., 2000. *Public participation in planning. New strategies for the 21st Century* [online]. University of California. Available from: http://escholarship.org/uc/item/3r34r38h [Accessed 16 November 2011].

Innes, J.E., Booher, D.E., and Di Vittorio, S., 2010. Strategies for megaregion governance: Collaborative dialogue, networks, and self-organization. *Journal of the American planning association*, 77 (1), 55–67.

IPCC, 2014. *Climate change 2014: Impacts, adaptation, and vulnerability*. IPCC WGII AR5 Chapter 23 [online]. IPCC. Available from: www.ipcc.ch/report/ar5/wg2/ [Accessed 22 July 2014].

Jacobs, J., 1961. *The death and life of great American cities*. New York, NY: Penguin Books.

Janssen, M., and Van der Voort, H., 2020. Agile and adaptive governance in crisis response: Lessons from the COVID-19 pandemic. *International Journal of Information Management*, 55, 102180.

Janssen-Jansen, L.B., 2004. *Regio's uitgedaagd. 'Growth Management' ter inspiratie voor nieuwe paden van pro-actieve ruimtelijke planning*. Assen: Van Gorcum.

Janssen-Jansen, L.B., and Tan, W., 2018. A Dutch perspective on urban growth boundaries. From containing to stimulating growth. In: J.-D. Gerber, T. Hartmann, and A. Hengstermann, eds. *Instruments of land policy. Dealing with scarcity of land*. Oxon: Routledge, 137–141.

Jiang, H., 2021. *Smart urban governance. Governing cities in the "smart" era*. Utrecht: Utrecht University.

Jiang, H., Geertman, S., and Witte, P., 2019. Smart urban governance: An urgent symbiosis? *Information Polity*, 24 (3), 245–269.

Jiang, H., Geertman, S., and Witte, P., 2020. A sociotechnical framework for smart urban governance. *International Journal of E-Planning Research*, 9 (1), 1–19.

Kearns, A., and Paddison, R., 2000. New challenges for urban governance. *Urban Studies*, 37 (5–6), 845–850.

Kiernan, M., ed., 2000. *Francis Bacon: The advancement of learning*. Oxford: Oxford University Press.

Kihlström, A., 2012. Luhmann's system theory in social work: Criticism and reflections. *Journal of Social Work*, 12 (3), 287–299.

Klemme, M., and Selle, K., eds., 2010. *Siedlungsflächen entwickeln. Akteure. Interdependenzen. Optionen*. Detmold: Rohn Verlag.

Knaap, T., and Oosterhaven, J., 2003. Spatial economic impacts of transport infrastructure investments, Chapter 5. In: A. Pearman, P. Mackie and J. Nellthorp, eds., *Transport Projects, Programmes and Policies: Evaluation Needs and Capabilities*. pp 87–105. Hampshire: Ashgate.

Knoepfel, P., *et al.*, 2011. *Public policy analysis*. Bristol, UK: Policy Press.

Koelman, M., Hartmann, T., and Spit, T.J.M., 2021. When tensions become conflicts: wind turbine policy implementation and development in the Netherlands. *Journal of Environmental Planning and Management*, 1–22. DOI: 10.1080/09640568.2021.1885018

Kreukels, A.J.M., 1985. Planning als spiegel van de westerse samenleving. *Beleid en Maatschappij* (12), 311.

Kreukels, A.M.J., 1997. *Een perspectief voor de stad*. Rotterdam: Van de Rhee.

Kreukels, A.M.J., and Wever, E., 1998. *North Sea ports in transition. Changing tides*. Assen, The Netherlands: Van Gorcum.

Lambregts, B., Janssen-Jansen, L., and Haran, N., 2008. Effective governance for competitive regions in Europe: the difficult case of the Randstad. *GeoJournal*, 72 (1–2), 45–57.

Lange, M. de, Mastop, H., and Spit, T., 1997. Performance of national policies. *Environment and Planning B: Planning and Design*, 24 (6), 845–858.

Lester, T.W., and Reckhow, S., 2013. Network governance and regional equity: Shared agendas or problematic partners? *Planning Theory*, 12 (2), 115–138.

Logan, J.R., and Molotch, H.L., 1987. *Urban fortunes. The political economy of place*. Berkeley, CA: University of California Press.

Macdonald, S., Monstadt, J., and Friendly, A., 2021. From the Frankfurt greenbelt to the Regionalpark RheinMain: An institutional perspective on regional greenbelt governance. *European Planning Studies*, 29 (1), 142–162.

Mastop, H., and Faludi, A., 1997. Evaluation of strategic plans: the performance principle. *Environment and Planning B: Planning and Design*, 24 (6), 815–832.

McGuirk, P., 2008. Building the capacity to govern the Australian metropolis. *Built Environment*, 34 (3), 255–272.

Meijer, M., 2018. *Community-led government-fed and informal. Exploring planning from below in depopulating regions across Europe*. Dissertation. Nijmegen: Radboud University.

Monstadt, J., 2007. Urban governance and the transition of energy systems: Institutional change and shifting energy and climate policies in Berlin. *International Journal of Urban and Regional Research*, 31 (2), 326–343.

Moroni, S., 2010. Rethinking the theory and practice of land-use regulation: Towards nomocracy. *Planning Theory*, 9 (2), 137–155

Mouat, C., and Dodson, J., 2013. Reviewing the Auckland 'super city': Towards an ongoing agenda for evaluating super city governance. *Australian Planner*, 50 (2), 138–147.

Needham, B., 1988. Continuity and change in Dutch planning theory. *Netherlands Journal of Housing and Environmental Research*, 3 (1), 5–22.

Needham, B., 2006. *Planning, law, and economics. The rules we make for using land*. Abingdon, Oxon: Routledge.

Needham, B., 2007. *Dutch land-use planning. Planning and managing land use in the Netherlands, the principles and the practice*. Den Haag: Sdu uitgevers.

Needham, B., 2014. *Dutch land-use planning. The principles and the practice*. Surrey, UK: Ashgate.

Needham, B., Buitelaar, E., and Hartmann, T., 2018. *Planning, law and economics. The rules we make for using land*. Abingdon, Oxon [UK]: Routledge.

Needham, B., and Hartmann, T., 2012. Conclusion. Planning by law and property rights reconsidered. In: T. Hartmann and B. Needham, eds. *Planning by law and property rights reconsidered*. Farnham: Ashgate, 219–227.

Needham, B., et al., 2000. *Kwaliteit, winst en risico. De invloed van het Vinex-onderhandelingsmodel op de programmatische ontwikkeling van Vinex-locaties*. Nijmegen, Utrecht.

North, D.C., 1990. *Institutions, institutional change, and economic performance*. Cambridge, New York, NY: Cambridge University Press.

Nuissl, H., and Heinrichs, D., 2011. Fresh wind or hot air — Does the governance discourse have something to offer to spatial planning?. *Journal of Planning Education and Research*, 31 (1), 47–59.

Paris, A., 2018. *Solving complex problems at the regional scale (master's thesis)*. Utrecht: Utrecht University. Available from: http://www.inplanning. eu/categories/12/articles/240?menu_id=omgevingswet&section_title_for_ article=Theses+Omgevingswet

Park, J., 2020. Changes in subway ridership in response to COVID-19 in Seoul, South Korea: Implications for social distancing. *Cureus*, 12 (4), e7668.

Parker, G., and Doak, J., 2012. *Key concepts in planning*. Los Angeles: SAGE Publications.

Patton, C.V., and Sawicki, D.S., 1986. *Basic methods of policy analysis and planning*. Englewood Cliffs, NJ: Prentice-Hall.

Peek, G.-J., Bertolini, L., and Jonge, H. de, 2006. Gaining insight in the development potential of station areas: A decade of node-place modelling in The Netherlands. *Planning Practice and Research*, 21 (4), 443–462.

Persson, T., Roland, G., and Tabellini, G., 1997. Separation of powers and political accountability. *The Quarterly Journal of Economics*, 112 (4), 1163–1202.

Pierre, J., 2005. Comparative urban governance: Uncovering complex causalities. *Urban Affairs Review*, 40 (4), 446–462.

Priemus, H., 2007. Development and design of large infrastructure projects: Disregarded alternatives and issues of spatial planning. *Environment and Planning B: Planning and Design*, 34 (4), 626–644.

Priemus, H., Nijkamp, P., and Banister, D., 2001. Mobility and spatial dynamics: An uneasy relationship. *Journal of Transport Geography*, 9 (3), 167–171.

Reimer, M., Getimis, P., and Blotevogel, H.H., eds., 2014. *Spatial planning systems and practices in Europe. A comparative perspective on continuity and changes.* New York, NY: Routledge.

Rhodes, R.A., 2007. Understanding governance: Ten years on. *Organization Studies*, 28 (8), 1243–1264.

Rietveld, P., and Nijkamp, P., 2000. Transport infrastructure and regional development. *Analytical Transport Economics. An International Perspective*, 208–232.

Rigney, D., 2010. *The Matthew effect. How advantage begets further advantage.* New York, NY: Columbia University Press.

Rittel, H.W., and Webber, M.A., 1973. Dilemmas in a general theory of planning. *Policy Sciences* (4), 155–169.

Roo, G. de, and Silva, E.A., eds., 2010. *A planner's encounter with complexity.* Farnham, Surrey: Ashgate.

Rotmans, J., Kemp, R., and Van Asselt, M., 2001. More evolution than revolution: Transition management in public policy. *Foresight*, 3 (1), 15–31.

Rydin, Y., 2010. Actor-network theory and planning theory: A response to Boelens. *Planning Theory*, 9 (3), 265–268.

Salet, W.G.M., Thornley, A., and Kreukels, A., 2003. *Metropolitan governance and spatial planning. Comparative case studies of European city-regions.* London, New York, NY: Spon Press.

Scharpf, F.W., 1997. *Games real actors play. Actor-centered institutionalism in policy research.* Boulder, CO: Westview Press.

Schmitt, P., and Smas, L., 2021. Ist die formelle Regionalplanung in Europa wirklich tot? *ARL Nachrichten*, 50 (3), 23–27.

Schmitt, P., and Wiechmann, T., 2018. Unpacking spatial planning as the governance of place: Extracting potentials for future advancements in planning research. *disP-The Planning Review*, 54 (4), 21–33.

Schofield, J., 2001. Time for a revival? Public policy implementation: A review of the literature and an agenda for future research. *International Journal of Management Reviews*, 3 (3), 245–263.

Schreuder, Y., 2001. The Polder Model in Dutch economic and environmental planning. *Bulletin of Science, Technology & Society*, 21 (4), 237–245.

Sclar, E., *et al.*, eds., 2020. *Zoning. A guide for 21st-century planning.* New York, NY: Routledge.

Selle, K., 2010. *Something went wrong. Vom langen Weg zur lokalen Beteiligungskultur* [online]. Available from: www.planung-neu-denken.de. [Accessed 1 November 2021]

Shahab, S., Clinch, J.P., and O'Neill, E., 2018. Accounting for transaction costs in planning policy evaluation. *Land Use Policy*, 70, 263–272.

Shahab, S., Clinch, J.P., and O'Neill, E., 2019. Impact-based planning evaluation: Advancing normative criteria for policy analysis. *Environment and Planning B: Urban Analytics and City Science*, 46 (3), 534–550.

Shaw, D., Nadin, V., and Westlake, T., 1995. The compendium of European spatial planning systems. *European Planning Studies*, 3 (3), 390–395.

Short, J., and Kopp, A., 2005. Transport infrastructure: Investment and planning. Policy and research aspects. *Transport Policy*, 12 (4), 360–367.

Silver, H., Scott, A., and Kazepov, Y., 2010. Participation in urban contention and deliberation. *International Journal of Urban and Regional Research*, 34 (3), 453–477.

Snel, K.A., 2021. Flooded with Expectations. Exploring the Perspectives of Residents at Flood Risk (dissertation). Utrecht: Utrecht University.

Snel, K.A.W., et al., 2019. More than a one-size-fits-all approach – tailoring flood risk communication to plural residents' perspectives. *Water International*, 44 (5), 554–570.

Snel, K.A.W., et al., 2020. The shifting position of homeowners in flood resilience: From recipients to key stakeholders. *Wiley Interdisciplinary Reviews: Water*, 7 (4), e1451.

Sohn, Y.J., and Edwards, H.H., 2018. Strategic ambiguity and crisis apologia: The impact of audiences' interpretations of mixed messages. *International Journal of Strategic Communication*, 12 (5), 552–570.

Spit, T., and Bertolini, L., 1998. *Cities on rails. The redevelopment of railway station areas*. London, New York, NY: E&FN Spon.

Spit, T., and Zoete, P.R., 2009. *Ruimtelijke ordening in Nederland. Een wetenschappelijke introductie in het vakgebied*. Den Haag: Sdu uitgevers.

Spit, T., and Zoete, P.R., 2016. *Planologie. Een wetenschappelijke introductie in de ruimtelijke ordening in Nederland*. [Groningen]: Coöperatie In Planning UA.

Spit, T.J., 1998. Ruimtelijke ordening. Integraliteit van beleid als probleem. *Bestuurswetenschappen*, 52 (6), 289–296.

Stephenson, P., 2013. Twenty years of multi-level governance: 'Where Does It Come From? What Is It? Where Is It Going?'. *Journal of European Public Policy*, 20 (6), 817–837.

Sternberg, E., 2000. An integrative theory of urban design. *Journal of the American Planning Association*, 66 (3), 265–278.

Stöglehner, G., 2020. *Grundlagen der Raumplanung – Strategien, Schwerpunkte, Konzepte*. Wien: Facultas.

Suprayoga, G.B., 2020. *Integrating sustainability into road infrastructure development. A dead-end street or a promising road?* Utrecht: Utrecht University.

Suprayoga, G.B., Witte, P., and Spit, T., 2020a. Identifying barriers to implementing a sustainability assessment tool for road project planning: An institutional perspective from practitioners in Indonesia. *Journal of Environmental Planning and Management*, 63 (13), 2380–2401.

Suprayoga, G.B., Witte, P., and Spit, T., 2020b. The sectoral lens and beyond: Exploring the multidimensional perspectives of sustainable road infrastructure development. *Research in Transportation Business & Management*, 37, 100562.

Tarlock, D., 2012. Global climate change and the stability of property rights. In: T. Hartmann and B. Needham, eds. *Planning by law and property rights reconsidered*. Farnham: Ashgate, 135–156.

Tarlock, D., and Albrecht, J., 2016. Potential constitutional constraints on the regulation of flood plain development. Three case studies. *Journal of Flood Risk Management*, 13 (11), 2379.

Taylor, N.M., 1998. *Urban planning theory since 1945*. London, Thousand Oaks, CA: SAGE Publications.

Teisman, G., Van Buuren, A., and Gerrits, L., 2009. *Managing complex governance systems*. Oxon: Routledge.

Tempels, B., and Hartmann, T., 2014. A co-evolving frontier between land and water: Dilemmas of flexibility versus robustness in flood risk management. *Water International*, 39 (6), 872–883.

Thiel, F., 2018. Regulatory or expropriatory? On the implications of the Transatlantic Trade and Investment Partnership for the German land policy. *Land Use Policy*, 77, 778–789.

Torfing, J., and Ansell, C., eds., 2016. *Handbook on theories of governance*. S.l.: Edward Elgar Publishing.

Vale, D.S., 2015. Transit-oriented development, integration of land use and transport, and pedestrian accessibility: Combining node-place model with pedestrian shed ratio to evaluate and classify station areas in Lisbon. *Journal of Transport Geography*, 45, 70–80.

Van Ark, R., 2005. *Planning, contract en commitment. Naar een relationeel perspectief op gebiedscontracten in de ruimtelijke planning*. Delft: Eburon.

Van den Hoek, D., Spit, T., and Hartmann, T., 2020. Certain flexibilities in land-use plans: Towards a method for assessing flexibility. *Land Use Policy*, 94, 104497.

Van Den Hof, G.J.J., 2006. *PPS in de polder: De betekenis van publiekprivate samenwerking voor de borging van duurzame ruimtelijke kwaliteit op Vinex-locaties* (Vol. 343). Utrecht: Utrecht University.

Van der Steen, M., 2017. Anticipation tools in policy formulation: Forecasting foresight and implications for policy planning. In: M. Howlett and I. Mukherjee, eds. *Handbook of policy formulation*. Cheltenham: Edward Elgar Publishing, 182–197.

Van der Valk, A., and Faludi, A., 1997. The green heart and the dynamics of doctrine. *Netherlands Journal of Housing and the Built Environment*, 12 (1), 57–75.

Van Dijk, T., Van Kann, F., and Woltjer, J., 2019. *Explaining Dutch spatial planning*. Groningen: InPlanning.

Van Oosten, T., Witte, P., and Hartmann, T., 2018. Active land policy in small municipalities in the Netherlands: "We don't do it, unless . . .". *Land Use Policy*, 77, 829–836.

Van Straalen, F.M., Hartmann, T., and Sheehan, J., 2018. Changing environmental conditions, property rights and land use planning. In: F. van Straalen, T. Hartmann, and J. Sheehan, eds. *Property rights and climate change. Land-use under changing environmental conditions.* Abingdon, Oxon [UK], New York, NY: Routledge, 1–10.

Van Straalen, F.M., Janssen-Jansen, L.B., and Van den Brink, A., 2014. Delivering planning objectives through regional-based land-use planning and land policy instruments. An assessment of recent experiences in the Dutch provinces. *Environment and Planning C: Government and Policy*, 32 (3), 567–584.

Van Straalen, F.M., and Witte, P.A., 2018. Entangled in scales: Multilevel governance challenges for regional planning strategies. *Regional Studies, Regional Science*, 5 (1), 157–163.

Van Straalen, F.M., Witte, P.A., and Buitelaar, E., 2017. Self-Organisation in Oosterwold, Almere: Challenges with public goods and externalities. *Tijdschrift voor Economische en Sociale Geografie*, 108 (4), 503–511.

Vigar, G., 2009. Towards an integrated spatial planning? *European Planning Studies*, 17 (11), 1571–1590.

Voogd, H., 1995. *Methodologie van ruimtelijke planning.* Bussum: Coutinho.

Vroom, L., and Van Straalen, F.M., 2016. Sustainable development: The role of scientific literature in Dutch municipal spatial planning. *Journal of Sustainable Development*, 9 (2), 193.

Waterhout, B., 2007. Episodes of Europeanization of Dutch national spatial planning. *Planning Practice and Research*, 22 (3), 309–327.

Wegener, M., 2012. Government or governance? The challenge of planning for sustainability in the Ruhr. In: T. Hartmann and B. Needham, eds. *Planning by law and property rights reconsidered.* Farnham: Ashgate, 157–168.

Wesselink, A., *et al.*, 2007. Dutch dealings with the Delta. *Nature & Culture*, 2 (2), 188–209.

Wildavsky, A., 1973. If planning is everything, maybe it's nothing. *Policy Sciences* (4), 172.

Witte, P., 2014. *The Corridor Chronicles. Integrated perspectives on European transport corridor development.* Delft: Eburon Academic Publishers.

Witte, P., and Spit, T., 2014. Sectoral drawbacks in transport: Towards a new analytical framework on European transport corridors. In: I.M. Lami, ed. *Analytical decision-making methods for evaluating sustainable transport in European corridors.* Cham: Springer International Publishing, 47–61.

Witte, P., *et al.*, 2018. Facilitating start-ups in port-city innovation ecosystems: A case study of Montreal and Rotterdam. *Journal of Transport Geography*, 71, 224–234.

Witte, P., Wiegmans, B., and Ng, A.K., 2019. A critical review on the evolution and development of inland port research. *Journal of Transport Geography*, 74, 53–61.

Wolsink, M., 2003. Reshaping the Dutch planning system: a learning process? *Environment and Planning A*, 35 (4), 705–723.

Yang, H., 2018. *High speed rail and urban networks in China (dissertation)*. Utrecht: Utrecht University.

Yang, H., *et al.*, 2019. Comparing passenger flow and time schedule data to analyse High-Speed Railways and urban networks in China. *Urban Studies*, 56 (6), 1267–1287.

Yiftachel, O., and Huxley, M., 2000. Debating dominance and relevance. Notes on the 'communicative turn' in planning theory. *International Journal of Urban and Regional Research*, 24 (4), 907–913.

Zoete, P.R., 1997. *Stedelijke knooppunten: Virtueel beleid voor een virtuele werkelijkheid? Een verkenning van de plaats van indicatief rijksbeleid in de wereld van gemeenten*. Amsterdam: Thesis Publishers.

Zonneveld, W., and Evers, D., 2014. Dutch national planning at the end of an era. In: M. Reimer, P. Getimis, and H.H. Blotevogel, eds. *Spatial planning systems and practices in Europe. A comparative perspective on continuity and changes*. New York, NY: Routledge, 61–82.

Index

active land policy 20, 31, 40, 42,
  62–63
actor-network theory 106
actor-relational planning 11,
  105–106
actors *see* stakeholders
administrative context of planning
  77–84
AESOP (Association of European
  Schools of Planning) 107–108
allocation 4, 9, 16–18, 36, 41, 60,
  78–85

Betuweroute 18, 51–52, 85, 100,
  106
blueprint planning 21, 27, 65–66,
  74–75
bottom-up 83
brownfield development 32
bundled deconcentration 28, 46
business sector *see* market

centralization 80–82, 84, 88–90
Central Place Theory 18
citizen participation *see* participatory
  planning
city extension 25–26, 28–29
civil society 19, 62, 66–67, 69, 81,
  102, 103
classic planning system *see*
  coordination structure
climate change 4, 6, 9, 24, 32, 44,
  71, 92–93, 95, 97, 100, 102, 106
collaboration 19, 23, 46, 72–73, 83,
  87, 101

collaborative planning *see*
  participatory planning
communication 19, 22–23, 67, 90, 96
communicative spatial planning 16,
  23, 28, 66, 74
compact city 28–29, 33, 49, 53
complexity 3, 6, 35, 36, 43–44,
  47–54, 64, 68, 70, 85, 95, 97–98,
  101, 102–103, 107
comprehensive planning 2–4, 9–11,
  20–21, 41, 53, 67–71, 88–89,
  101
concept *see* spatial planning concept
conservation planning 41–42
context 1, 17, 19–20, 23–24,
  31–32, 34, 77–98, 101–103,
  106–107
contraction 42
coordination structure 31, 67,
  69–71, 84, 92, 97
corridor development 51–52, 85, 100
COVID-19 *see* pandemic
critical infrastructures 36, 91
cumulative effects 93–94

decentralization 81–84, 88
demographic development 4, 24, 32,
  59, 93–94
Derde Nota see Third Memorandum
development-led planning 41–42
digitalization 24, 106–107
dilemmas 16–20, 68–69, 97
distribution issues 18, 26, 40, 44,
  53–54, 81–86, 94
dynamics 9, 47–48, 70, 89, 103

economic collapse 6, 9, 20, 28, 31–32, 39
energy transition *see* transitions
Environment and Spatial Planning Act 10, 19, 32, 34, 71–72, 81, 89, 92, 98
equivalence principle 78–82
European Union 13, 45
ex ante evaluation 64, 75
expansion 7, 29, 52, 70
ex post evaluation 58, 63

facilitating land policy 31, 63
Fifth Memorandum 30–31
financial crisis *see* economic collapse
financial flows 81–82
flexibility 85–86
formal planning system *see* coordination structure
Fourth Memorandum 29
Fourth Memorandum Extra 28–30, 46, 54
future 5–12, 25, 96, 106
futuring 6

garden cities 25
Gebundelde deconcentratie see bundled deconcentration
globalization 32, 70, 93
Goedhart doctrine 78–82
governance 19, 51, 64–75, 95, 101, 106–107
greenfield development 26, 29, 32, 42, 68
Green Heart 18, 26–29, 46, 84, 106
growth management 26, 42, 52

healthy cities 6, 9

implementation 1, 5, 9, 12–14, 19, 42, 51, 62–63, 66, 73–74, 89–91, 100
incentives 16, 31, 46
infrastructure development 7, 12, 18, 36, 42, 48–54, 94–95
institutional context of planning 84, 97
institutional theory 20
institutional void 70, 83
institutions 23, 38, 44, 70–71, 86

integrality *see* comprehensive planning
integrated planning *see* comprehensive planning
intermunicipal planning *see* regional planning

land development 44, 55, 68
land market 9, 18, 31, 37–40
land policy 1–2, 20, 31, 62–63, 107–108
land servicing 44
land use 17–18, 37–48, 53–54, 58
land use plan 17, 40, 45–47, 62–63
land use planning 4–5, 32, 53–54, 94–95
land valuation 36
legal certainty 5, 9, 40, 85–86, 92
legislation 9, 12–13, 47, 74, 92, 97
legitimacy 16, 19, 24, 57–58, 83, 87, 101
Leidsche Rijn 29–30, 42
localization 93–94
location 16, 19–20, 37–39, 44–46

mainports 29, 33, 56, 105
managed growth *see* growth management
market 11, 19, 28–30, 47, 57, 62–63, 65–67, 69, 74–75, 85, 89, 93, 102, 103
Merwedekanaalzone 32–33
mirror of society 4, 20, 22, 31, 53, 77, 96, 104
mobility-as-a-service 7, 17, 32
mobility transition *see* transitions
multi-level *see* dynamics
municipality 6, 9, 20, 31, 45, 60, 62–63, 68, 71–72, 78–85, 88–91, 96–97

National Environmental Vision 34, 72, 100
national government 31–32, 46, 68, 71, 74, 78–85, 88–91, 96–97
National Memorandum 31
new town development 26
Nieuwegein 27–28
NIMBY 50, 59

normativity 6–7, 75–76, 91, 100–103
Nota Ruimte see National Memorandum
NOVI *see* National Environmental Vision

object 17–18, 21–23, 34, 36–55, 92, 99–101, 103–104
Omgevingswet see Environment and Spatial Planning Act
open planning process 23–24, 64–67, 71–75, 101–103
operational planning 68, 71, 74

pandemic 24, 39, 92–93, 95–97, 102
participation *see* participatory planning
participatory planning 11, 19, 21–23, 65–69, 81, 87–88, 101
passive land policy 20, 62–63
performance 85, 89–91, 97, 99–100
policy cycle 12, 57–64
policy implementation 12, 57, 89–91
policy objectives 60–61, 90–91, 100
plan design 61–62
plan-making process *see* plan preparation
planner 61, 66, 73–75
Planner's Paradise 2, 28
planning *see* spatial planning
planning concept 26, 28–29, 33, 46, 64
planning context 20, 102–103
planning doctrine 2, 18
planning intervention 14, 18, 20, 35, 53, 60, 62, 65
planning law 2, 18, 25, 84, 87
planning methods 6, 19, 108
planning theory 15–16, 18–21, 34, 86, 101
planning traditions 4–5
planning triangle 2–4, 16–17, 34–35, 99–102
planning process 18–19, 22–23, 56–76, 101
planning studio 15
planning support science 6

planning system 2, 35, 45, 47, 67, 71, 74, 76, 78, 84–85, 92, 97
plan preparation 57, 61, 64
post-modern planning 22, 106
private sector *see* market
process *see* planning process
process planning *see* planning process
projective scenario 5–7
property rights 14, 19, 38, 86–87, 95
prospective scenario 5–7
provinces 30–31, 45, 68, 70–74, 81–85, 88, 90, 96–97
public activity 5, 11, 19
public interest 7–9
public-private partnerships 28, 30, 66

Randstad 18, 26, 29, 46, 53, 84, 94, 106
rational-comprehensive planning 22, 43
real estate market 6, 31, 37–40, 50, 92
reconstruction 21, 102
regional development 53
regional gap 83
regional governance 70–73, 84
regional planning 17, 46, 70–73, 82–83
regional policy 82
regulation 13, 17, 39–40, 42, 47, 62, 72, 74, 86–87, 92, 97, 99
resilience 18, 86, 95, 100
Rijnenburg 32–33, 68

satellite town 27–28
scale 19, 25, 44–50, 52–54, 68–73, 92–93
scarcity 9, 18, 36–37, 39, 43, 53–54, 58, 84, 86, 95
scenarios 5–7, 19, 25, 61
Second Memorandum 26
sectoral planning 9–11, 14, 17, 43, 57, 88, 101
sectoral policy 68, 80
self-organization 11, 81
situational land policy 20, 31
smart cities 92, 100, 107
societal development 20, 31, 48, 54, 77, 92–96, 102, 104, 106
spatial design 44, 80

spatial planning 1–108
spatial planning concept *see*
  planning concept
spatial planning system *see* planning
  system
spatial scales *see* scale
stakeholders 3, 7, 11, 14, 17, 19,
  22, 43, 45, 53, 56–57, 59–75, 86,
  87–88, 90–91, 100, 104–106
state 9, 12–13, 45, 101–103
strategic planning 3, 36, 41, 68, 74, 106
*Structuurvisie Infrastructuur en
  Ruimte* 31
subsidiarity principle 45, 47, 80–81,
  88–89, 96–97
sustainability 6–7, 18, 68, 92, 100,
  103, 106–107

tensions 5, 58, 72, 81, 84–89, 94
third aspiration level 78–80, 82
Third Memorandum 28, 33
top-down 83, 90–91, 101
transitions 20, 24, 32, 83, 92, 100,
  102, 106–107
transit-oriented development 17, 30,
  46, 48

trias politica 11–13, 78
Tweede Nota see Second
  Memorandum

uncertainty 5, 41, 50, 92–93,
  95–96, 100–103, 107
urban densification 29, 32, 53
urban networks 49
urban nodes 29
urban planning 40, 95, 105
urban transition *see* transitions
Utrecht school 99, 104

Vijfde Nota see Fifth Memorandum
Vinex see Fourth Memorandum
  Extra
Vinex locations *see* Fourth
  memorandum Extra
Vino see Fourth Memorandum

Wet op de Ruimtelijke Ordening 31
wicked problems 22–23, 35, 59, 61,
  71, 102–103
WRO/Bro 25

zoning 4, 39–41, 47, 56, 71, 101

For Product Safety Concerns and Information please contact our EU
representative GPSR@taylorandfrancis.com
Taylor & Francis Verlag GmbH, Kaufingerstraße 24, 80331 München, Germany